Moses' Rock

IRISH DRAMATIC TEXTS

MOSES' ROCK

By Frank O'Connor
and Hugh Hunt

Edited
with an Introduction and Notes
by
Ruth Sherry

The Catholic University of America Press
Washington, D.C.

Colin Smythe
Gerrards Cross, Bucks.

Library of Congress Cataloging in Publication Data

O'Connor, Frank, 1903–1966.
  Moses' Rock.

  (Irish dramatic texts)
  I. Hunt, Hugh, 1911–   . II.Sherry Ruth.
III. Title. IV. Series.
PR6029.D58M6 1983   822′.912   82-23478
ISBN 0-8132-0584-0
ISBN 0-8132-0585-9 (pbk.)

British Library Cataloguing in Publication Data

O'Connor, Frank
  Moses' rock.—(Irish dramatic texts)
  1. Title   II. Hunt, Hugh
III. Sherry, Ruth   IV. Series
822′.914   PR6029.D58

  ISBN 0-86140-182-4
  ISBN 0-86140-183-2 P6K

CONTENTS

ACKNOWLEDGEMENTS

Most grateful thanks are due to the following, who have shared their knowledge and resources with me: Brendan Kennelly, J. J. Finegan, Nicholas Grene, Nathaniel Healy, Elizabeth Malcolm, Margaret O'Brien, Maurice Sheehy and Richard Walsh. Heartfelt thanks as well to Magni Ljoså for help which, as usual, extended well beyond the call of duty. Without the encouragement and exertions of Hugh Hunt and Harriet Sheehy, publication of this volume would have been literally impossible, but each deserves, in addition, my special thanks for unfailing graciousness and generosity.

CHRONOLOGY

(This chronology gives a detailed account of Frank O'Connor's life and major publications, and a briefer view of the main events in Hugh Hunt's career.)

1903   Michael Francis O'Donovan born 17 September in Cork, son of Michael O'Donovan and Minnie O'Connor O'Donovan; later formed his pseudonym Frank O'Connor from his own middle name and his mother's family name.

1911   Hugh Hunt born 25 September.

1918   O'Connor became active in the Volunteers.

1922   Resisting the Treaty, O'Connor served in the IRA; his first poems published in *An Long*, a Cork Republican newspaper.

1923   O'Connor captured by government forces, interned at Gormanstown army camp, Co. Meath.

1924   O'Connor trained as librarian in Sligo.

1925   O'Connor worked as librarian in Wicklow; first publication in *The Irish Statesman,* under the pseudonym Frank O'Connor.

1926   O'Connor took up post as librarian in Cork.

1928   O'Connor active as producer with the Cork Drama League.

1929   O'Connor took up post as librarian at Pembroke Library, Angelsea Road, Dublin.

1931   O'Connor's first book, *Guests of the Nation* (stories), published.

1932   O'Connor's *The Saint and Mary Kate* (novel) and *The Wild Bird's Nest* (poems from the Irish), published.

1933   Hunt became President of Oxford University Dramatic Society.

1934   Hunt received B. A., Oxon. Worked as producer at Maddermarket Theatre, Norwich, later at Croydon Repertory and Westminster Theatres (until 1935).

1935   Hunt appointed as producer at the Abbey Theatre, August. O'Connor appointed to Board of Directors of the Abbey Theatre, October.

1936   O'Connor published *Three Old Brothers* (poems); *Bones of Contention* (stories).

1937   Hunt's adaptation of O'Connor's story, "In the Train," produced at the Abbey, 31 May. *The Invincibles,* by Hunt and O'Connor, produced at the Abbey, 18 October. O'Connor published *The Big Fellow* (biography of Michael Collins), began broadcasting for the BBC.

1938   *Moses' Rock* produced at the Abbey, 28 February. O'Connor retired from library service to work full time as a writer; moved to Woodenbridge, Co. Wicklow; published *Lords and Commons* (poems from the Irish). Hunt left the Abbey, November, to produce Paul Vincent Carroll's *The White Steed* in New York. O'Connor's *Time's Pocket* produced at the Abbey, 26 December.

1939   O'Connor married Evelyn Bowen Speaight, 11 February; resigned as Director of the Abbey Theatre, May; published *The Fountain of Magic* (poems from the Irish); son, Myles, born. Hunt entered military service in Britain, served until end of World War II.

1940   O'Connor published *Dutch Interior* (novel), banned in Ireland; *Lament for Art O'Leary* (poem from the Irish); daughter, Liadain, born. First issue of *The Bell* published, October; O'Connor served as its poetry editor until 1943.

1941   O'Connor moved to Dublin with his family; published *Three Tales* (stories); his play *The Statue's Daughter* produced by the Dublin Drama League at the Gate Theatre, 8 December.

1942   O'Connor's father died 20 March.

1943   O'Connor began writing social and political criticism for the *Sunday Independent* under the pseudonym Ben Mayo, continued until 1945; *A Picture Book* (travel) published.

1944   O'Connor worked in England for the Ministry of Information; published *Crab Apple Jelly* (stories).

1945   O'Connor published *Towards an Appreciation of Literature* (criticism); *The Midnight Court* (poem from the Irish), banned in Ireland in 1946; his son, Oliver, born in England to Joan Knape. Hunt became director of Bristol Old Vic Company.

1946   O'Connor's *Selected Stories* published; son, Owen, born to Evelyn.

1947   O'Connor published *Irish Miles* (travel); *The Art of the Theatre* (criticism); *The Common Chord* (stories), banned in Ireland.

1948   O'Connor published *The Road to Stratford* (criticism).

1949   O'Connor separated from Evelyn, moved to England. Hunt became Director of the Old Vic Company, London.

1950   O'Connor published *Leinster, Munster and Connaught* (travel); lived between Dublin and England.

1951   O'Connor's *Traveller's Samples* (stories) published, banned in Ireland.

1952   *The Stories of Frank O'Connor* published. O'Connor divorced from Evelyn; taught in the USA at Northwestern and Harvard Universities; his mother died 10 November.

1953   O'Connor married Harriet Rich of Annapolis, Maryland, in England, 5 December.

1954   O'Connor's *More Stories* published; he lived between Ireland and USA hereafter. Hunt's *Old Vic Prefaces* and *The Director in the Theatre* published; he served as Adjudicator of the Canadian Drama Festival Finale.

1955   Hunt became Executive Officer of the Elizabethan Theatre Trust, Australia; served until 1960.

1956   O'Connor published *The Mirror in the Roadway* (criticism) and *Stories by Frank O'Connor.*

1957   O'Connor published *Domestic Relations* (stories) and *Modern Irish Short Stories* (anthology).

1958   O'Connor's daughter Harriet born.

1959   O'Connor published *A Book of Ireland* (anthology); *Kings, Lords and Commons* (poems from the Irish), banned in Ireland in 1961.

1960   Hunt's *The Making of the Australian Theatre* published.

1961   O'Connor's *An Only Child* (autobiography) published. Hunt appointed Professor of Drama, University of Manchester.

1962   O'Connor awarded D. Litt. from Trinity College, Dublin; *The Lonely Voice* (criticism) published. Hunt's *The Live Theatre* published.

1963   O'Connor's *The Little Monasteries* (poems from the Irish) and *My Oedipus Complex and Other Stories* published.

1964   O'Connor lectured at Trinity College, Dublin; published *Collection Two* (stories).

1966   O'Connor died 10 March, buried in Deans Grange Cemetery, Dublin.

1967   O'Connor's *The Backward Look* (literary history) and *A Golden Treasury of Irish Poetry A. D. 600–1200* (translations, with David Greene) published. *The Invincibles* revived at the Abbey, 4 September.

1968   O'Connor's *My Father's Son* (autobiography) published.

1969   O'Connor's *Collection Three* (stories) and *A Set of Variations* (stories) published. Hunt appointed Artistic Director of the Abbey, served until 1971.

1973   Hunt retired from professorship at University of Manchester.

1975   O'Connor's *The Statue's Daughter* published.

1977   Hunt awarded C. B. E. (Commander of the Order of the British Empire.)

1979   Hunt's *The Abbey: Ireland's National Theatre 1904–1979* published.

1980   *The Invincibles* published. Hunt's *Sean O'Casey* published.

1981   O'Connor's *The Cornet Player Who Betrayed Ireland and Other Stories* and *Collected Stories* published.

NOTE ON DOCUMENTATION

Many of O'Connor's works were published both in Britain and/or Ireland and in the United States — not necessarily simultaneously. Dates given in the foregoing Chronology are for first publication, regardless of where it occurred. However, references to the texts in the footnotes to the Introduction cite American editions where these exist; some apparent discrepancies of date therefore occur. For detailed bibliographical information on O'Connor's writings, see *Michael/Frank*, ed. Maurice Sheehy (New York, 1969.) References in the footnotes to works by writers other than O'Connor likewise cite American, rather than British or Irish, editions wherever possible.

INTRODUCTION

Biographical information

page 26 Moses

I

Frank O'Connor was a dominant figure in the generation of Irish writers whose careers began at about the same time that Ireland achieved independence from Britain in the early 1920's. O'Connor's adolescence coincided with the closing phases of the Irish struggle for independence. In this hopeful period, O'Connor, like many other imaginative young people, expected that political self-determination would open up boundless possibilities for a cultural and spiritual transformation of Ireland. Unprecedented artistic fulfillment would be at hand once the nation was free to express its identity in its own way.

The realities of life in Ireland after independence proved disillusioning for O'Connor, as for many other artists and writers, but he always retained the sense that it was his task to explore all aspects of his country's life and history, both as an artist and as a citizen. As a result, O'Connor had a remarkably varied career. Although he is now best known as a writer of short stories, O'Connor was also in the course of his career a self-taught scholar and translator of older Irish poetry; he was a librarian, a novelist, a poet, a literary critic and historian, a biographer and autobiographer, a writer of travel

1

books which placed particular emphasis on architectural history, a columnist commenting on the current political and social scene, a broadcaster, a theatrical producer and administrator, a drama critic and a dramatist. This last aspect of his career is not among the most familiar, since he wrote only four plays, and none of these was published during his lifetime, yet his plays reflect some of his persistent concerns as a writer and as an Irishman, and they have a place in the history of Irish literature and drama.

Like many another young writer, O'Connor initially thought of himself as a lyric poet. His inclinations in this direction were encouraged partly by his devotion to the dominating literary figure of the previous generation, W. B. Yeats, whom O'Connor met in 1925 at the beginning of his professional career. For O'Connor, however, writing poetry was always an activity which tended to merge with another of his passions, the study of the Irish language, and his lyric impulse ultimately found its most satisfying expression, not in poems of his own composing, but in translations of older Irish poetry into English. A striking feature of the poems O'Connor chose to translate is that they often tend toward the dramatic mode, and even in his earliest translations he was particularly successful at conveying the sense of an immediate situation, and of a strong and personal voice speaking:

> Woman full of wile
> Take your hand away
> Nothing tempts me though
> Sick for love you pray.
> See this hair how greyed!
> See this flesh, how weak!
> See this wasted blood!
> —Tell me what you seek.[1]

There is a similar tendency toward the dramatic in the poetry of Yeats himself, and many have felt that there is something in Irish culture which encourages this particular note in its literary expression. Certainly Ireland retained a vital oral tradition, of verse-speaking, ballad-singing, and story-telling, for far longer than most other Western European nations, and this tradition has left its mark on the modern literature, even

---

1. "Autumn," in *The Wild Bird's Nest* (Dublin, 1932), p. 11.

though it is produced for quite different circumstances of appreciation.

Although he concentrated on poetry at this early stage in his career, O'Connor was also trying his hand at the short story, and this genre, with its realistic rather than romantic and lyrical orientation, ultimately proved to be his most natural mode of expression. But the same distinctive, personal speaking voices, the same sense of immediacy which had marked many of his original poems and translations, soon emerged in the short stories:

"I've another little story for you," said the old man.

"I hope it's a good one," said I.

"The divil a better. And if you don't believe me you can go down to Courtenay's Road and see the truth of it with your own two eyes. Now it isn't every wan will say that to you?"

"It is not, then."[2]

O'Connor later had considerable success as a reader of his own stories on the radio, and observed in connection with this experience that he "was horrified to discover how the written word had robbed the story of its narrative impulse. For some years I concentrated on putting [it] back. . . . Generations of skilful stylists from Chekhov to Katherine Mansfield and James Joyce had so fashioned the short story that it no longer rang with the tone of a man's voice, speaking."[3]

It seems inevitable, then, that a writer fascinated with "the tone of a man's voice, speaking," and with a sense of tension and immediacy central to much of his poetic and narrative writing, would sooner or later try his hand at the literary form which offers the most complete expression for such impulses, the drama. But there were other circumstances which also encouraged O'Connor's experiments as a dramatist.

The last years of the nineteenth century, and the first years of the twentieth, are now familiarly labelled "The Irish Renaissance"; the period saw the flowering of a literature which was deliberately and distinctively Irish, rather than merely provincially "West British," in its subject matter and language, and to some extent in its literary forms. Lasting achievements

---

2. "The Late Henry Conran," in *Guests of the Nation* (New York, 1931), p. 244.

3. "Foreword," *Stories by Frank O'Connor* (New York, 1956), vii.

were made in poetry, especially by W. B. Yeats, and in fiction, especially by James Joyce, but the most striking and distinctive contribution of the movement as a whole was in the drama. The creation of Ireland's national theatre, the Abbey, encouraged the development of a distinctively Irish tradition of acting and production, and gave a home for plays written by Irish writers, preferably using Irish subject matter, and, when possible, written in the Irish language. Major literary figures, including Yeats, George Moore, and George Russell (AE), tried their hands at drama even though none of them was primarily a dramatist, and other writers, including Lady Gregory, J. M. Synge, and, in later years, Sean O'Casey, developed into dramatists of world stature. By the time Frank O'Connor reached adulthood, the Abbey Theatre was an established force in the cultural life of Ireland, and in many ways it appeared to be the most significant achievement of a cultural nationalism which, if not always explicitly political in its motivation, nevertheless had made its contribution toward the definition of an independent Irish nation. Taking the theatre into account thus became natural for many young Irish writers, even those whose major gifts lay elsewhere. O'Connor was one of these.

The Abbey Theatre was however part of the Dublin world, while O'Connor was from Cork, and did not establish himself in the Dublin milieu until he was in his mid-twenties. O'Connor's earliest mentor was another Corkman, Daniel Corkery (1878–1964), who was himself a writer of stature, and was O'Connor's first teacher of Irish. Corkery had some experience as a dramatist and theatrical producer, and he was also responsible for introducing O'Connor to the work of the Russian writers. Anton Chekhov in particular became one of O'Connor's models and life-long ideals. Chekhov is perhaps the only writer of world stature whose reputation is based almost equally upon his contributions to the drama and to the short story; certainly his example could help to spur a young writer achieving success in one genre to try his hand at the other. After O'Connor met Yeats, in 1925, he was provided with another powerful model and also with a source of contact with Dublin's theatrical milieu, for during the last four decades of his life Yeats directed almost as much attention to the writing of plays and the running of the Abbey Theatre as he did to writing poetry.

In his autobiography, *An Only Child*, O'Connor describes how, as a child, he made a model theatre and constructed miniature performances, largely for his own edification.[4] Yet despite this precocious interest in the theatre, his first practical association with the stage seems to have come in 1928 when, having made the acquaintance of the Dublin literary world, he had returned to Cork to work as a librarian, and founded the Cork Drama League. He was significantly involved here in three productions, including one of Chekhov's *The Cherry Orchard*, and there is evidence that he was trying his own hand as a dramatist at about the same time, anticipating production with the Cork Drama League, but these efforts were cut short by his decision to take a post as librarian in Dublin at the end of 1928.[5] In the years that followed he had ample opportunity to attend the Dublin theatres and he fell increasingly under the sway of Yeats, who, searching for allies, was in October 1935 instrumental in having O'Connor appointed to the Board of Directors of the Abbey Theatre. Before long O'Connor took on significant administrative responsibilities in the theatre, and in the climate of the Dublin of the time, the limits of his practical experience seemed unimportant beside the fact that he was being accorded increasing recognition for his work as a short story writer, translator and critic; that he should be engaged in running a world-famous theatre seemed a natural outgrowth of his position as a man of letters.

In the 1930's O'Connor shared many of his developing ideas about literature and the theatre with another Cork-born, Corkery-trained young writer, Sean O'Faolain. The two helped to educate each other in continental literature, and the works of modern European dramatists naturally figured in

---

4. *An Only Child* (New York, 1961), p. 153.

5. The Cork Drama League was an amateur organization which did not long survive O'Connor's departure for Dublin at the end of 1928. He gives an account of its activities in *My Father's Son* (New York, 1969), Ch. 7. In a letter to Sean O'Sullivan, O'Connor refers to having written "a three-act comedy about the Civil War" for the League, and mentions other, short, plays "long since scrapped." (Letter of 2 March [1928], Trinity College Dublin MS 3940, my date.) Another, unidentified play is referred to in a letter to O'Sullivan of 5 April 1929 (Trinity College Dublin MS 884.)

their reading and thinking. They debated, both in private and in public, what kind of theatre would best suit the national and artistic needs of Ireland; they were concerned that the work of native Irish dramatists should be fostered, but they wanted Ireland at the same time to remain open to foreign influences so that provincialism would be avoided. One issue was whether the Abbey should produce non-Irish plays, another was how much emphasis should be given to encouraging work in the Irish language.[6]

Under the circumstances, it was virtually inevitable that O'Connor should become active as a dramatist. His first play was not, however, an independent effort, but a collaboration with the Abbey's producer, Hugh Hunt. Hunt was a young Englishman who had worked successfully as a producer in several English theatres; he was appointed at the Abbey on the suggestion of Yeats, who was interested in providing the theatre with a more cosmopolitan outlook. Hunt took up his post at the Abbey only a few months before O'Connor was appointed as a Director, and he had a practical and technical knowledge of the theatre which O'Connor lacked. Hunt's dramatization of one of O'Connor's short stories, "In the Train," was produced at the Abbey in May 1937.[7] The two cooperated so successfully on this venture that they went on to collaborate on an original play, *The Invincibles*, which was the first of three plays in which O'Connor was to explore major events in the struggle for Irish independence in the latter half of the 19th century. *The Invincibles* was produced at the Abbey in October 1937, a few weeks before Sean O'Faolain's first and only play, *She Had to Do Something*, appeared there with a young Welsh actress in the leading role. She was Evelyn Bowen, the wife of the rising English actor and writer, Robert Speaight. As she was not Irish and was relatively inexperi-

---

6. See, for example, letter by O'Connor and O'Faolain, *The Irish Times*, 25 February 1935; O'Faolain's "The Abbey Theatre," *The Irish Times*, 20 and 21 September 1938; letter by O'Connor, *The Irish Times*, 3 October 1938; letter by O'Faolain, *The Irish Times*, 6 October 1938; letters by O'Connor and O'Faolain, *The Irish Times*, 12 October 1938.

7. The text of Hunt's dramatization was not published until long after O'Connor's death. In the meantime O'Connor himself wrote his own dramatization of the same story. See Hugh Hunt, *In the Train* (New York, 1973) and Frank O'Connor, "In the Train," in *The Genius of the Irish Theatre*, ed. S. Barnet, M. Berman and W. Barto (New York, 1960), pp. 245–261.

enced, the casting of Evelyn Bowen in a leading role in Ireland's national theatre was controversial, and the controversy surrounding her did not diminish when, a few months later, she and her son went to live in Co. Wicklow with O'Connor, who resigned his post as a librarian. The relationship with Evelyn Bowen gave O'Connor yet another tie with the theatre, but it shocked many people, at the Abbey and elsewhere, and diminished the degree of authority and good-will O'Connor enjoyed in the theatre. In 1939, when Evelyn's divorce from Speaight became final, she and O'Connor were married. At the end of February, 1938, *Moses' Rock* (another O'Connor-Hunt collaboration) was produced. The following November, Hunt left the Abbey to take up a post elsewhere, already well embarked upon what became a distinguished international career in the theatre.[8] O'Connor's third historical play, *Time's Pocket*, was therefore completed without Hunt's collaboration. This play, unlike the earlier ones, was not particularly well received, and O'Connor and O'Faolain defended it in rather arrogant terms in a series of letters in the major Dublin newspapers.[9]

W. B. Yeats, who had protected O'Connor in his exposed position at the Abbey, died early in 1939. O'Connor himself, in *My Father's Son*, gives a rather bitter account of the events which followed in the next few months, implying that he was being driven out of the theatre partly because of his private life and partly because he attempted to uphold the theatre's artistic standards, in the tradition of Yeats, while other members of the theatre's Board were prepared to sacrifice these standards to considerations of political expediency.[10] O'Connor resigned from his managerial post, ostensibly over the issue of allowing external censorship of the theatre's productions, in May 1939,[11] although he retained a

---

8. Hunt has given an account of his own relationship with the Abbey in his history of that theatre, *The Abbey: Ireland's National Theatre 1904–1979* (New York, 1979.) Hunt's work for the Abbey is praised in *My Father's Son*.

9. Others, including the then-unknown Flann O'Brien, contributed to the controversy in the Letters to the Editor columns of the Dublin newspapers. See *The Irish Times*, 6, 11, 13, 14, 16, 17, 18, 19, 21, and 30 January and 1 February 1939; *The Irish Independent*, 6, 7, 10, 11, 12, 14, 16 and 18 January 1939.

10. *My Father's Son*, Part IV.

11. See *The Irish Press*, 5 May 1939.

limited connection with the theatre for some time thereafter. However, severing connections with the Abbey left him with no showcase for his own plays.

O'Connor and O'Faolain devoted considerable energy to plans for providing Irish dramatists with an alternative to the Abbey as an outlet for their work, and attempted to engage other important Irish writers, such as Denis Johnston and Elizabeth Bowen, in these efforts, but the practical results of their efforts proved short-lived. O'Connor's last play, *The Statue's Daughter*, was eventually produced at the Gate Theatre under the auspices of the Dublin Drama League in December 1941.[12] Whether the loss of immediate contact with the theatre was the major cause of O'Connor's giving up his efforts as a dramatist, or whether he needed a collaborator, like Hugh Hunt, with a better grasp than his own of the practicalities of dramatic production, can scarcely be determined. He and O'Faolain began to collaborate on a dramatization of the life of Parnell, but nothing came of the project.[13]

Yet O'Connor never lost interest in the theatre or in dramatic literature. A series of lectures given at Hull University in 1945 were published under the title *The Art of the Theatre*.[14] In 1947 *The Road to Stratford*, a study of Shakespeare, was published, and this work was revised as *Shakespeare's Progress* in 1960;[15] O'Connor's approach to theatre in general, and to Shakespeare in particular, is partly informed by his own direct, practical experience of the theatre. In the 1950's he served for a time as theatre critic for *Holiday* magazine, and he published an article on acting as late as 1963. His second autobiographical work, *My Father's Son*, left unpublished at the time of his death in 1966, devotes much attention to his years at the Abbey

---

12. The Dublin Drama League was founded in 1918. Its initial aim was to complement the Abbey's work by producing non-Irish plays, although it later presented some Irish plays as well. The League was active from 1919 to 1929 and was revived in 1936 and 1941. *The Statue's Daughter* was one of the last plays produced under its auspices. For a more detailed account, see Brenna Katz Clarke and Harold Ferrar, *The Dublin Drama League 1918–1941* (Dublin, 1979.)

13. O'Connor's and O'Faolain's plans for the Parnell play and for an alternative to the Abbey Theatre are found in letters now held in the O'Connor papers, Mugar Library, Boston University, and in the O'Faolain papers, Bancroft Library, University of California, Berkeley. Revival of the Dublin Drama League figured in these plans.

14. *The Art of the Theatre* (Dublin, 1947).

15. *The Road to Stratford* (London, 1948); *Shakespeare's Progress* (New York, 1960).

Theatre, while his history of Irish literature, *The Backward Look*, also posthumously published, includes thoughtful assessments of the major dramatists of the Irish Renaissance.[16]
Although an interest in drama and the theatre thus persisted throughout O'Connor's lifetime, his active career as a dramatist was, as we have seen, confined to a period of about five years in the late 1930's and early 1940's. This period was one of transition for O'Connor as a writer, and a play like *Moses' Rock* in fact looks both backward and forward. O'Connor's stories of the 1930's tend to deal with war, with life in the slums of Cork, and with the relationship between modern Ireland and Gaelic Ireland—all subjects which are taken up by one or more of his plays. By the early 1940's, however, he had tended to move on to other subjects—notably life in provincial towns, and the romantic and domestic problems of young people. These are subjects which his last three plays also treat, but only in combination with a consideration of politics and history—matters which ceased to have such strong interest for O'Connor after the early 1940's. (Still later in his career O'Connor was to achieve singular success with stories of childhood and with sympathetic treatments of the lives of priests, but there is little sign of any interest in these themes in the work of the late 1930's.) O'Connor's plays thus provide an interesting perspective on his career, and a unique combination of themes and interests seen elsewhere in his more familiar work.
All of O'Connor's plays deal with political events as they resound in individual lives, and each is centered on the figure of a heroic nationalist. Three of the plays, including *Moses' Rock*, look back to significant events in nineteenth-century Irish history, while the fourth, *The Statue's Daughter*, deals rather with the aftermath of the struggle for Irish independence as reflected in a modern provincial town. O'Connor's concern with Irish political history was clearly affected by his own involvement, in his late adolescence, in the last phases of that struggle.
Under the influence of Daniel Corkery, and with the support of his mother, O'Connor at about the age of fifteen had

---

16. American edition, *A Short History of Irish Literature: A Backward Look* (New York, 1967.)

joined the Volunteers, a loosely-organized but extensive guerrilla force which used all means at hand to attempt to force
the British to give up control of Ireland. When the British in
1921 signed a treaty with the Provisional Government of Ireland, establishing the Irish Free State, O'Connor was one of
many who refused to accept the Treaty. As it did not give the
Irish government control over Ulster, and as it provided for
a limited form of connection with the British crown, the
Treaty did not satisfy all the aspirations of those who had
aimed to achieve an independent and unified Republic of Ireland. Many formed the Irish Republican Army (IRA) and continued the guerrilla warfare, now not against the British, but
against those who had been their own comrades-in-arms but
now adhered to the Free State. O'Connor was briefly engaged
in combat; early in 1923 he was captured by government
forces, imprisoned for a time, and then interned in an army
camp for several months until the Republican resistance col-
lapsed and most Republicans agreed to acknowledge the le-
gitimacy of the Free State Government.[17]

His experiences in the Volunteers and in the IRA provided the seed for many of O'Connor's early stories and the
focus of his first book, *Guests of the Nation* (1931). Many of
these stories raise serious questions about political idealism,
the use of violence, and the relationship between private and
public postures. O'Connor's experiences in prison and in an
internment camp had altered his outlook. One thing he observed was that private and personal worth bore little relationship to any particular political commitment. An "enemy"
might prove kinder and more congenial than a "comrade," an
Englishman more admirable than an Irishman. Insights like
these find expression in O'Connor's single most famous story,
"Guests of the Nation." "Soirée Chez Une Belle Jeune Fille"
and "The Patriarch" explore the theme that human sympathies
cut across political boundaries; "Jo" and "Jumbo's Wife" raise
the disturbing problem that political "commitment" may be
turned to serve private ends. "Alec" and "Attack" raise the
possibility that violence and destructiveness themselves, rather
than any political ideal, are what primarily attract certain characters to a "cause."

---

17. *An Only Child*, Part IV.

His re-evaluation led O'Connor to something close to a complete rejection of his previous convictions as a Republican. As a mature man, he tended to see his own political involvement as a product of naiveté and excessive romanticism; he espoused instead the alternative values of commitment to private relationships. Increasingly, he insisted upon judging the effect of actions as well as the principles they were based upon, and he evaluated individuals by their accomplishments and character, rather than by their proclaimed devotion to a particular cause. These values are suitably coupled, in O'Connor's stories, with an emphasis on characterization and a commitment to the depiction of actual, rather than idealized, experience. These tendencies, realistic rather than romantic, are also reflected in O'Connor's plays.

But by the time he began writing plays, O'Connor, like many other young Irishmen, had become disillusioned on more than one score. Whatever the limits of his youthful devotion to Republicanism, that devotion had been based upon something other than a mere commitment to a particular constitutional system. Before independence was achieved, "the Republic" tended to be a loose but glorious concept capable of sheltering a multitude of aspirations, not all of which were mutually compatible. For some it implied a new social justice, for others the opportunity to get money into their own pockets at last; for some it implied spiritual freedom, for others the opportunity to impose a particular sectarian culture and morality on the whole country.

The fact that an actual republic was not achieved, constitutionally speaking, until 1948, is irrelevant. The point, for O'Connor and many others, was that independence did not bring the gains—cultural, economic or spiritual—which they had envisioned. Looked at in one way, this state of affairs made youthful enthusiasm, like O'Connor's, seem naive and misguided. Looked at in another, it might seem that the Irish nation had proved itself unworthy of the labors, sacrifices, and suffering of its leaders and patriots. Both of these notes are struck in O'Connor's plays, each of which presents the image of a heroic nationalist whose compatriots prove themselves unworthy of his courageous, even sacrificial, efforts on their behalf.

11

II

O'Connor's interest in exploring and re-evaluating his own stance during the Civil War had also led him to a direct consideration of historical figures. In particular, he became fascinated by Michael Collins, one of the military leaders of the Volunteers, and conceived a great admiration for him which he expressed in the form of a book, *The Big Fellow*, which was published in 1937,[18] the same year O'Connor's first play was produced. The study of historical persons was of course a natural outgrowth of a critical interest in Irish politics and history; his friend, O'Faolain, wrote studies of several earlier nationalist leaders, notably one of Daniel O'Connell, the first great Catholic political leader of modern times. And, while there was no particularly strong Irish tradition of using historical material as the subject of drama, other writers, including Sean O'Casey, Denis Johnston, and Lady Gregory had already done so. Inevitably, one figure, that of Charles Stewart Parnell, had exerted a fascination, not only upon dramatists, but upon other creative writers of O'Connor's generation and the one which just preceded it.

Parnell was the single dominating figure of Irish political life in the last quarter of the nineteenth century. In the course of his parliamentary career he brought Irish hopes for the peaceful achievement of a significant degree of self-government to an unprecedented pitch; his fall from power scotched these hopes, and Irish self-determination was finally achieved only at the price of bloodshed and enduring bitterness. Parnell's career has therefore been a central theme for historians; as an individual he has proved intriguing to creative writers, and his fall, in particular, has been seen as a turning point of more than merely political significance. A powerful but aloof and enigmatic figure during his lifetime, Parnell took on mythical dimensions after his death, and his fall came to be seen as an event of symbolic import.

Parnell, like many other Irish nationalist leaders of the eighteenth and nineteenth centuries, was of Anglo-Irish Protestant, rather than Catholic Gaelic, stock. He owned a substantial estate, Avondale, near Rathdrum in Co. Wicklow.

---

18. American edition, *Death in Dublin* (New York, 1937).

Then, as now, it was neither necessary nor particularly common for a member of the British parliament to be a resident of the district he represented. Parnell was first elected as Member of Parliament (MP) for Meath in 1875. In the general election of 1880 he took the perfectly permissible course of standing for election for three different seats, one for Meath, one for Mayo, and one for Cork. He won all three contests and chose to take the seat for Cork, which he then held until his death in 1891.

Ireland was represented by just over 100 members (the number varying slightly from time to time) for most of the nineteenth century, and the Irish members constituted about one-sixth of the total. For the greater part of the century, these Irish members had tended to reflect a variety of interests, and they sided individually with one or another of the dominant British parties in the various matters which arose. By the early 1870's, however, a number of Irish MPs were elected essentially because they were committed to some considerable degree of political self-determination for Ireland. Parnell was not the first to perceive that these MPs collectively would very often hold the balance of power in the House of Commons, but he was the first to make effective use of the fact.

Irish MPs of nationalist inclination had various short and long-term goals. The most important of these concerned land reform and self-government. Most Irish farmers, whether small or large, did not own the land they worked, but rented it from landlords (of whom Parnell himself was one) with little or no long-term security of tenure. An immediate aim was to guarantee that tenant farmers could not be arbitrarily evicted from their holdings at short notice, and that the rent they paid should be reasonable and predictable. The long-term aim was that the land should be owned by those who worked it. As for self-government, Ireland had for centuries had its own parliament, and for a brief but glorious period (1782–1800) this parliament exercised virtually complete control over Ireland's internal affairs. The Irish parliament was, however, abolished in 1800 (partly because of a bloody but abortive rebellion in 1798) and Ireland's internal affairs were thereafter controlled, along with its external affairs, by the British parliament at Westminster in London. Here, MPs for Ireland were always in a substantial minority and Irish matters were accorded comparatively little attention.

Some Irish nationalists wanted complete independence for Ireland, with total control of all internal and external affairs and a republican form of government like that established in the United States and in France as the result of revolutions. There were various shades of opinion between these and those who would have settled for a much more limited form of "Home Rule," in which Ireland's internal affairs would be run independently from Dublin, but she would still be united with Britain under the same sovereign and have her foreign affairs conducted by the authorities in London. However, even those who held to the republican ideal generally supported Home Rule as a first step along the road to it.

Historically, there had long been a conflict between Irishmen who believed that one or both of these major goals, land reform and political independence, could be achieved purely by political activity, and those who held that nothing short of "physical force" would ever produce decisive results. Although Parnell from time to time gave at least tacit support to various groups and individuals who were prepared to use violent methods, his main achievement was to establish that parliamentary politics could produce genuine advances by methods which were peaceful, if not necessarily orthodox. On most occasions, notably after the politically-inspired murder of the Chief Secretary for Ireland and his assistant in 1882, Parnell denounced the use of terrorist methods. (These murders provided the subject of the play *The Invincibles* by Hugh Hunt and Frank O'Connor.)

In Parliament Parnell began to achieve power, less by oratorical skill or maneuverings in the corridors, than by gradually asserting a quality of peculiar stubbornness and determination. His aristocratic air of implacability and self-sufficiency was combined with a complete indifference to the established rules of the parliamentary game. Parnell employed a variety of techniques to gain power for the Irish party; the most notorious of these was a form of filibuster, in which he and other Irish MPs held the floor uninterruptedly and thereby prevented the transaction of business which was irrelevant to Ireland. Parliamentary rules were in time changed to allow for closure of debate but by this point Parnell had successfully served notice on the two major British parties, the Liberals and the Conservatives, that the Irish party could act in a unified fashion under his leadership, and that the party would not permit the House of Commons to function unless Irish interests were given adequate attention. From this point on it became a matter of which of the British parties could offer the most to Parnell in the way of Irish reforms, in exchange for support on other matters.

In the period from 1875 to 1891, the most notable achievement of the Irish Parliamentary Party was the passage of a series of Land Acts which made notable, although gradual, changes in the circumstances of Irish farmers. A persistent problem was eviction of tenant farmers from farms on which they had lived for many years. Evictions occurred when poor farmers could not pay unfairly raised rents, or when even wealthy farmers refused to pay them as a matter of policy. The Land League, of which Parnell was nominally a leader, attempted to devise techniques for forcing land reforms and caring for evicted tenants. Some of these techniques could be regarded as extreme, and the authorities' response was often severe.

For a long period in 1881–2, Parnell was in fact imprisoned in Kilmainham Jail in Dublin for what the authorities claimed was incitement to violent action over land issues; his public speeches certainly indicated that Parnell felt the government was not willing to go far enough in its concessions to Irish farmers. Parnell was released from prison after he agreed not to continue to speak out against a particular Land Act, but he made this agreement only in exchange for promises of further reforms.

Episodes of this kind served to reinforce the sense that Parnell was a leader of an unprecedented kind. He could bring the British around by exploiting the possibilities implicit in the parliamentary situation, but he was also capable of employing the time-honored Irish technique of forcing concessions by voluntarily enduring great hardship. After his release from Kilmainham in 1882, Parnell exerted an authority which was virtually beyond question. People began to speak of him as "The Uncrowned King of Ireland."

Parnell's eventual fall from power had little effect on land reform, which was substantially achieved by the time he disappeared from the political scene. What was devastating was the effect of his fall on Irish hopes of Home Rule. Although Parnell had always been prepared to bargain with either of the British parties, the leader of the Liberal Party, W. H. Gladstone, himself became essentially convinced of the rightness of Irish demands for reform, and it was from Liberal governments that the Irish had the most to hope for. The Liberals lost power in the General Election of 1886, but in the latter part of 1890 it was anticipated (incorrectly, as it turned out) that another election would be held before long, and it seemed likely that the Liberals would then be returned to power. Parnell, after protracted negotiations, had virtually won from Gladstone a guarantee that the next Liberal government would, as an early priority, introduce a Home Rule Bill which would guarantee Ireland a substantial, if not unlimited, degree of self-government. This was the goal for which Parnell had labored during the whole of his parliamentary career, but it was at this point that the catastrophe occurred.

In 1890, at the age of 43, Parnell was still a bachelor. A proud man, formal and distant even with close associates, he ostensibly had no intimate relationships except with his own immediate family. Yet in fact Parnell had, since 1880, been involved in a liaison with Katharine O'Shea, the estranged wife of Captain William O'Shea, a small-time Irish politician of few abilities but great ambitions. For at least part of the period O'Shea had been well aware of his wife's relations with Parnell, to whom Katharine had borne three children. O'Shea in fact owed his seat in parliament to Parnell, who had engineered O'Shea's election over the protests of other, more reliable, members of his party. The relationship between Parnell and Mrs. O'Shea had become more and more of an open secret during its latter years, but it is still a matter of debate why O'Shea, who had tolerated, and indeed profited from, his wife's association with Parnell for so many years, should at length have decided to sue her for divorce, naming Parnell as co-respondent. The best estimate is that his reasons were probably financial.

The divorce case, which was tried in November 1890, was the scandal of the decade, perhaps of the century. Under the law of the time, a decree of divorce was awarded only if there were one guilty and one innocent party. If both husband

and wife were shown to be guilty of marital wrongdoing, the marriage would stand. It had been Parnell's desire for many years to marry Katharine and live with her openly. Therefore, he and Mrs. O'Shea decided not to defend themselves in court. To prove either that O'Shea had accepted their relationship, or that he had himself been anything but a faithful husband, would have meant that no divorce would be granted. O'Shea was awarded his divorce, and Parnell finally married Katharine on 25 June 1891—but politically he was doomed.

It was fairly clear to politicians that the cause of Home Rule could be seriously damaged by having as its chief spokesman a man who, in effect, was publicly "convicted" of adultery. Parnell's force of character and leadership ability were, however, such that the Irish MPs at first feared that losing him as leader might be even more damaging to the cause than retaining him, despite the stain on his character.

A meeting of the Irish party was held on 25 November 1890, and by unanimous vote Parnell was retained as party leader. It was not long, however, before W. H. Gladstone, largely out of respect for non-Conformist moral opinion in Britain (which provided the major part of his own support), declared that he could not continue as leader of a Liberal Party committed to Home Rule, if Parnell were to continue as leader of the Irish party. This move made the situation much more difficult for the Irish MPs; to many of them it now appeared to be a choice between the person of Parnell and the possibility of achieving Home Rule. A long and bitter meeting of the Irish party went on for a week at the beginning of December. The result was that the party split, with a majority of members voting to depose Parnell. In effect, Ireland now had two significant political parties, both committed to Home Rule. These soon became known as the Parnellite and the Anti-Parnellite parties.

Parnell responded to this defeat by attempting to take his case directly to the people of Ireland, trusting that his enormous personal popularity would ensure that he regained his former unquestioned position of leadership. He travelled to Ireland as soon as practicable after his defeat, and addressed crowds of supporters in both Dublin and Cork shortly after his arrival. He also—by main force—reasserted his control over the party newspaper, *United Ireland*, which had come out against him immediately after the party split. But his leadership was in fact lost forever. In the few months which remained of his life, three Irish seats in the House of Commons became vacant. Each of the resulting by-elections—at Kilkenny in December 1890, at Sligo in April 1891, and at Carlow in July 1891—was fought bitterly by Parnellite and Anti-Parnellite forces, and in each case the latter won. Parnell himself travelled extensively in Ireland during these months, visiting the country almost every weekend, both to campaign for his candidates in the by-elections and to attempt to recapture his rapidly diminishing popularity. The incessant travelling and strain doubtless contributed to undermining his health, which had been poor for years, and he died unexpectedly at home in Brighton with Katharine on 6 October 1891.

It is part of the received myth about Parnell's fall and death that he was killed by the Catholic bishops who had—in the most hostile version of the story—merely been waiting for the first opportunity to dethrone a Protestant as political leader of the largely Catholic population of Ireland. In fact, as recent studies demonstrate, clerical opinion about Parnell and his leadership was always somewhat divided. It is true that Irish bishops did issue statements to the faithful, including the "Bishops' Manifesto" of November 1890, in which they condemned Parnell and declared him morally unfit for the leadership of the Irish people. Many of these pronouncements were, however, made only by small groups of bishops, and most of them did not appear until after Parnell had already sustained fatal losses on the political front. While historical opinion is at present divided on the question of how important clerical opinion was as a factor in Parnell's fall, Gladstone and English non-Conformist moral opinion were almost certainly far more decisive factors.[19]

Although Parnell fell from power, he never lost his following completely. Those who remained loyal to him even after the Carlow by-election were, naturally enough, the most fiercely loyal, and Parnell's untimely death evoked in them both bitterness and a sense of tragic irony. J. H. Horgan, who

---

19. For differing evaluations of clerical responsibility for Parnell's fall, see F. S. L. Lyons, *Charles Stewart Parnell* (London, 1977), and Emmet Larkin, *The Roman Catholic Church in Ireland and the Fall of Parnell, 1888–1891* (Chapel Hill, North Carolina, 1979.)

was a child at the time, remembered how Cork responded to the news of "the Chief's" death:

> All Ireland stood aghast at the tragic news. The life of the country seemed to have ceased with him. In Cork, business was paralyzed, shops closed, strong men cried in the streets. Even his political enemies stood dismayed at this frightful climax to their campaign against him. He had died, as he promised, fighting to the end. My father came home that night utterly broken down. I had never seen him cry before and it was terrible to see.[20]

Parnell's body was brought to Ireland from England for burial on 11 October, and great crowds met the boat and followed the body to Glasnevin cemetery in Dublin where it was buried. During the burial ceremony, a star fell—an event to which many assigned a more than natural significance. The fact that the body was not publicly displayed before burial doubtless contributed to a legend which arose shortly afterward to the effect that Parnell had not really died, that the coffin held either stones or someone else's body, and that Parnell himself had gone into hiding and would return to rescue Ireland at some future point of crisis.

The Irish parliamentary party did not lack leaders after Parnell's death, but the split within the party had destroyed its effectiveness. With their energies dissipated by internal quarreling, the Irish MPs failed to capitalize on Gladstone's good will, even though he became Prime Minister from 1892 to 1894. The Liberal leader, himself an old man at the time of Parnell's death, died in 1898. No Home Rule bill was passed by the British Parliament until 1914, and its implementation, postponed because of World War I, was superseded by the Irish rising of Easter 1916 and the Anglo-Irish War which followed. When the first decisive form of Irish independence was achieved by treaty between Britain and Ireland in 1921, it was in many ways more radical than anything Parnell had ever hoped to achieve. On the other hand, this treaty left unsolved the problem of Ulster, which haunts both Ireland and Britain to this day.

It is of course not possible to divine what would have happened to Ireland if Parnell had never fallen from power—

---

20. *Parnell to Pearse* (Dublin, 1948), pp. 49–50.

and indeed his health was so precarious that he might not have lived long in any case—but his fall and death have continued to hold the Irish imagination precisely because they give rise to so many might-have-beens. The most famous literary treatment of this subject is that found in James Joyce's *A Portrait of the Artist as a Young Man* (1916) with its account of a Christmas dinner destroyed by a hysterical quarrel over the recently-dead Parnell. The novel subtly expresses the sense that, in Ireland, heroes like Parnell can expect to be the objects of fanatical hatred or fanatical love, rather than just and considered appreciation. In the short story "Ivy Day in the Committee Room" (1914), Joyce presents the spectacle of a venal collection of political hangers-on who ostentatiously honor the anniversary of Parnell's death at the same time that their political attitudes and machinations constitute a denial of all that Parnell represented.

The other great figure of the Irish Renaissance, W. B. Yeats, tended, for all his differences with Joyce, to regard Parnell in a similar light. Like Joyce, he saw Parnell as a man too great for the nation which betrayed him. Yeats tended to associate the downfall of Parnell with an observation made by Goethe in a completely different context: "The Irish seem to me like a pack of hounds, always dragging down some noble stag."[21] In this way, Parnell became for Yeats a kind of political counterpart to J. M. Synge, whom Yeats regarded as the consummate artist, vilified and hounded to death by a public whose "nationalism" and "morality" masked ignorance, narrow-mindedness and spite. Parnell, like Synge, could be paralleled with others whom Yeats admired as noble figures who had attempted to serve Ireland and were thwarted by the very people they sought to serve. Addressing the ghost of Parnell, Yeats associates him with Hugh Lane,

> A man
> Of your own passionate serving kind who
> . . . has been driven from the place,
> And insult heaped upon him for his pains,
> And for his open-handedness, disgrace;
> Your enemy, an old foul mouth, had set
> The pack upon him.
> ("To a Shade," September 29, 1913)

---

21. *The Trembling of the Veil*, in *Autobiographies* (London, 1927), p. 390. See also *My Father's Son*, p. 138.

It is this note, most powerfully struck by Joyce and Yeats, of seeing the fall of Parnell as significant, not merely because of its historical importance, but also because it is the quintessential illustration of a persistent pattern of failure on the part of the Irish nation, which is the keynote of the most important literary treatments of Parnell, including those of O'Connor and Hunt.

An identification of Parnell with Moses had occurred at a fairly early stage in Parnell's career; the parallel between the enslaved Israelites on the one hand, and the colonized and oppressed Irish on the other, was obvious enough. To identify the figure of Parnell with Moses was perhaps particularly attractive because Parnell, as a member of the Anglo-Irish ascendancy, could be thought of as having been raised in the bosom of the oppressor, like the foundling Moses, an Israelite brought up in the very household of the Egyptian king. When Parnell's downfall became imminent, another parallel with Moses presented itself, even to him personally: Moses led his people out of bondage, but was not privileged to lead them into the freedom of the Promised Land; after forty years of wandering in the desert, he died on a hillside in view of the goal. The ironic implications were apparent for a Parnell who was deposed just as victory seemed within grasp for the Home Rulers.[22]

The earliest of several dramatic treatments of Parnell was "The Deliverer" written by Lady Gregory in 1911; this work was an allegorical elaboration of the identification of Parnell with Moses.[23] The action of Lady Gregory's play is ostensibly set in Biblical Egypt, but, lest anyone should miss the point, the Israelite slaves have such Irish names as Dan, Ard and Malachi. The Parnell/Moses figure is not named, but known only as "the King's Nurseling." The play centers on the Nurseling's discovery that he is not Egyptian but Israelite by birth. Although he is hailed as a potential savior by the Israelites, some jealousy of him is found in their ranks, and when he identifies with them by discarding his royal garments and appearing in the rags of a slave, he is rejected by most of his

22. See F. S. L. Lyons, "The Parnell Theme in Literature," in *Place, Personality and the Irish Writer*, ed. Andrew Carpenter, *Irish Literary Studies* I (New York, 1977.)

23. First produced 12 January 1911; published in *Irish Folk-History Plays*, Second Series (New York, 1912), pp. 143–183.

own people. Caught between the pettiness of the Israelites and the brutality of the Egyptians, the Nurseling is destroyed. The ending of the play echoes the legends to the effect that Parnell had never really died. Mistaken for a slave and severely beaten by a guard, the Nurseling appears to be dead, yet a figure rises from the place where his body is lying and stumbles away: is it the Nurseling in his own body, or is it merely his spirit? In 1911 the notion that Parnell was waiting somewhere in hiding to return at a moment of crisis was one which still had currency and a degree of credibility, as Lady Gregory pointed out in her afternote to the published play.

Like all allegories, that in "The Deliverer" is inexact. On the one hand there is no parallel to Mrs. O'Shea in the play, and it therefore avoids the issue of the extent to which Parnell caused his own downfall; on the other hand both Moses and Parnell led their people on the road to freedom in a way the King's Nurseling never does in Lady Gregory's play.

The emphasis of "The Deliverer" is rather on the problem of the identification between the leader and his people. Doubtless her own position as Irish, but also Protestant, titled, and land-holding, made Lady Gregory especially sensitive to the tensions experienced by persons of her own class who held nationalist sentiments and thereby identified themselves with a cause which was fundamentally that of the overwhelmingly Gaelic and Catholic population. One point of Lady Gregory's play seems to be that a man like Parnell was particularly exposed, his class and religion overshadowing his services to the nationalist cause once the crisis came.

"The Deliverer" is not one of Lady Gregory's most successful plays, perhaps because the implicit polemic is generally ill-suited to her talents. It was followed a few years later by a much more familiar and theatrically successful work, Lennox Robinson's *The Lost Leader*, which also employed the legend that Parnell did not really die.[24] In this play, an elderly man, living in seclusion in an isolated hotel, has always been believed by a young woman to be her mad uncle, brought back from America by her father at about the time of Parnell's death.

---

24. First produced 19 February 1918 at the Abbey Theatre; published at Palmerston Gardens, Dublin, 1918. The play was revived at the Abbey in August 1937 in a production directed by Hugh Hunt.

When the old man suffers a shock, it becomes clear that he either really is Parnell, or in his madness believes that he is— but he dies before his claim can be adequately tested.

Robinson's play, produced early in 1918, was written in a period of national crisis, and expresses more directly than Lady Gregory's the sense of Parnell as an unexcelled leader whose powers are needed by a confused nation which has found no replacement for him. The play is not interested in the truth or falsity of the legend that Parnell did not really die in 1891; rather, it uses this legend and the hopes aroused by the possibility of the return of Parnell to express a longing for someone of Parnell's power and authority to lead Ireland through the dark time which descended with Easter 1916.

Both Lady Gregory and Lennox Robinson avoided a direct representation of the historical Parnell in their plays, partly, no doubt, because both were writing at a time when many living people—including, not least, Mrs. Parnell— could remember the man himself too well for an actor's portrayal to be altogether convincing. A later generation did not feel the same constraints, and two plays, written shortly before *Moses' Rock*, are based upon a fairly realistic presentation of crucial events in Parnell's life: W. H. Fearon's *Parnell of Avondale* (produced in 1934)[25] and Elsie Schauffler's *Parnell* (produced in 1935).[26] Both plays begin with scenes which show Katharine O'Shea shortly before her first meeting with Parnell, and both end with Parnell's death. Schauffler's play gives rather more emphasis to the love affair than to Parnell's political life, and this in itself provides her play with a degree of internal unity, but in general both plays, although faithful to historical fact, suffer from failing to note Aristotle's observation that a play is not dramatically unified merely because it deals with events in the life of one man.

By far the most interesting forerunner to *Moses' Rock* is Seamus O'Kelly's *The Parnellite*, a seriously flawed work

25. First produced at the Abbey Theatre, 2 October 1934; published in Dublin, 1937. The play was revived at the Abbey in October 1935 in a production directed by Hugh Hunt.

26. This play was first produced in New York, 11 November 1935 and was published there in 1936. It was also produced in London on 23 April 1936. A film, starring Clark Gable and Myrna Loy, was made from this play in the same year. The play was first produced in Dublin at the Torch Theatre on 1 March 1937.

which nevertheless has much vitality and freshness.[27] Of all the Parnell plays, it is the only one which invites serious comparison with *Moses' Rock* because it, like *Moses' Rock*, is not so much interested in Parnell himself as in the impact of his career on the lives of ordinary citizens. Like *Moses' Rock* after it, *The Parnellite* presents a group of people (here, two families) who appear to be united politically at the outset but who take divergent courses as Parnell's career progresses and then collapses. Division over politics leads to the estrangement of two brothers, a proposed marriage fails to come about, neighbors who once supported the protagonist during an ordeal of imprisonment turn against him when he remains loyal to the fallen Parnell. The fact that similar episodes occur in *Moses' Rock* does not necessarily establish that O'Kelly's work influenced O'Connor and Hunt directly,[28] but it does reflect a continuing popular memory of the split and its effects, which were by no means confined to the politicians.

Parnell himself does not appear in *The Parnellite*. The central character is however a man in the Parnell mold: proud, unyielding, sure of his own righteousness, he is in the end destroyed, indeed killed, because of these qualities. He becomes a popular hero when, like Parnell, he serves a term of imprisonment because of his defiant activities in support of the Land League, but, also like Parnell, he is rejected and reviled at the end of the play. The most interesting character in *The Parnellite* is however a priest, who is indeed shown as turning against Parnell but is nevertheless treated with great sympathy. Mindful of the needs of his people, he is progressive but wary of radicalism, under pressure from every side and responsive to all the conflicting claims which the situation places upon him. He emerges neither as hero nor as victim, but as a beleaguered, decent man attempting to trace a path through a moral jungle. O'Kelly's play is too melodramatic in its approach to have survived as a living drama, yet it is an honest and thoughtful attempt to explore the implications of Parnell's fall without being bound by the standard preconceptions, and Hunt and O'Connor's work is written in the same spirit.

27. First produced at the Abbey Theatre, 24 September 1917; published at Naas [1919].
28. *The Parnellite* was in fact revived at the Abbey in May 1935.

As we have seen, Frank O'Connor never completed a play in which Parnell appears on stage as a major character, but he is used as an important offstage figure in both of the plays on which O'Connor collaborated with Hugh Hunt. The first of these, *The Invincibles*, is the only one of O'Connor's four plays which presents a direct dramatization of historical personages and events.[29] The subject of *The Invincibles* is the Phoenix Park murders of 1882 in which the newly arrived Chief Secretary for Ireland, Lord Frederick Cavendish, and his assistant, T. H. Burke, were killed in Dublin's Phoenix Park by a secret society of extreme nationalists known as "The Invincibles."[30] The action of the play concentrates, not on the murder itself, but on the Invincibles' motives and plans for the murder, its aftermath, and the imprisonment and execution of the two men who actually wielded the knives, Joe Brady and Tim Kelly. In the background lies the agitation over the Land Question; British intransigence on this issue contributed much to the Invincibles' sense of desperation.

As is often the case with O'Connor's Civil War stories, an essential concern of *The Invincibles* is the problem of the motives which lie behind political engagement. The play repeatedly poses the question, "Who is *really* devoted to Ireland?" Despite the urgency of the issues at hand, throughout the play one character or group after another is exposed as having shoddy motives or inadequate resolve. By the end of the play, only Joe Brady is shown as having acted consistently and single-mindedly in the conviction that what he does will help Ireland. Yet even Brady has acted in error, unaware that one of his victims is Cavendish, who is widely regarded as a potential peacemaker, and that the murders will be repudiated by the whole nation.

Brady is opposed in the play, not by any other character who can match his stature, but by the unseen figure of Parnell. When the play opens, Parnell is imprisoned in Kilmainham Jail for land agitation. In the course of the play he is released, having come to terms with Gladstone, and the Invincibles

---

29. *The Invincibles*, first produced at the Abbey Theatre, 18 October 1937; published ([Newark, Del.], 1980).

30. The organization's full name was "The Irish National Invincibles." A thorough treatment can be found in T. Corfe, *The Phoenix Park Murders* (London, 1958.)

quarrel among themselves as to whether his action has pre-empted the violent move they plan to make. One accuses another of being a fanatic who "won't accept the realities of the situation"[31]—namely that Parnell's methods are more effective than those the Invincibles have envisioned. After the murders, Parnell denounces those responsible, and any hope the Invincibles have of being supported by the country at large is thereby lost.

Joe Brady in *The Invincibles* is seen as a tragic character. His honesty, bravery and devotion are unquestioned, but, by contrast with Parnell, he comes to seem hotheaded and imprudent. Unlike Parnell, Brady is unable to conceive of negotiation and is unable to distinguish between sympathetic and hostile Englishmen. Joe Brady's tragedy is that he has, in his own time at least, chosen the losing side of the conflict between those committed to negotiation and those convinced of the need for violence. Lacking Parnell's sophistication, Brady takes the demands of nationalism literally, but is rejected by the very people he conceives himself to be acting for: "What did Parnell and the rest want if 'twasn't murder? Why did they talk to us of our wrongs. . . . Why only that they wanted us to strike back?"[32] To him, it is Ireland, not he, who is at fault; she has failed to give a clear message to her defenders. Brady's approach to death, in particular, is presented as noble, yet the play is informed by a realization that history, on the whole, has rejected his methods and applauded those of Parnell.

III

While O'Connor and Hunt use the figure of Parnell to make a crucial thematic point in *The Invincibles*, he has only a tangential relationship to the historical events upon which the play focuses. In *Moses' Rock*, he is equally unseen, but the play is structured on the curve of his downfall, which triggers crucial changes in the private relationships presented in the play. The play is shaped so that each act coincides with a particular phase in the last months of Parnell's life; Act One takes place on the day in December 1890 when the Irish Party deposed him at

31. *The Invincibles*, p. 24.
32. *The Invincibles*, pp. 72–73.

Three, Parnell is dead and disagreement has turned into violence. Joan, on the eve of her wedding to Coghlan, sees no bearable future for herself in Ireland and flees with her English lover to a more open and liberal life elsewhere.

An era of political confusion and ineffectuality has begun, represented particularly by Joan's father, a quintessential trimmer, about to stand for election (for Parnell's seat, presumably) despite the fact that his only conceivable qualification is his wealth. Joan's aunt, concluding the play, makes Joan's flight symbolic of a more general loss: "All that is young and beautiful is leaving Ireland now, like seagulls flying into the dark."

If Joan's disillusionment follows a curve parallel to the fall of Parnell, there is another, though less pronounced, movement in the opposite direction, as two cynical middle-aged characters, Joan's Aunt Kate and the family friend Dr. Jackson, emerge from their self-imposed emotional isolation, moved by their growing love for Joan and their realization that politics—on which they had both previously turned their backs—will bring about changes and suffering in her young life. The presence of these two characters at the end of the play tempers the prevailing sense of disillusion and despair with such consolation as is provided by a mature and unselfish assessment of "the realities of the situation."

Perhaps it is possible to find allegorical overtones in *Moses' Rock*, and to see Joan as representing Ireland, like the Ireland of the Jacobite ballads. In these, Ireland was often pictured as a woman waiting for her own true love, the deposed Catholic king of England, James II (or one of his descendants), to come and rescue her from desolation; sometimes she was pictured as surrounded by false or unworthy admirers, or even as mated to a clown. Joan's—or Ireland's—problem is that the men of her own country who claim to be devoted to her are in various ways unworthy. Through Hegarty and Coghlan the play suggests that Ireland lacks men who are adequate to both the political struggle and the domestic demands which will become paramount in a time of peace and freedom. Dr. Jackson is, surprisingly, more in love with Joan than any of the young men, but, just as he becomes a Parnellite only after Parnell has fallen, he fails to approach Joan before it is too late. Although he is the most acute and intelligent observer in the play, his inability to commit himself at the right moment condemns him to ineffectuality. Through him the play seems to suggest that Ireland's best—her intellectuals, sophisticates and free-thinkers in particular—have too long held themselves aloof from her struggles and have in essence left Ireland, like Joan, nowhere at home to turn for a worthy helpmate. Like Ireland in the Jacobite ballads, Joan must look over the water for her rescuer.

Fortescue, the man whom Joan chooses, is unacceptable in her Cork milieu, not only because he represents English domination but because he—like Parnell—has had a relationship with a married woman. In choosing Fortescue, Joan is acknowledging the emptiness of all the claims that have traditionally been made upon her. Hegarty prefers his friendship with Coghlan to his love for her—why should she be bound by faithfulness? Her father and Coghlan subordinate political loyalty to personal advancement—why should her choice of husband be limited by political considerations? It is a priest, Coghlan's brother, who is behind the violence which erupts in the play—why should she heed the voices of conventional morality?

The inadequacy of Joan's Irish suitors provides an implicit contrast with the unseen figure of Parnell, who was passionate in his devotion to his lady (unlike Hegarty) and resolute even in defeat (unlike Coghlan). In Yeats's words, "Parnell loved his country, and Parnell loved his lass."[35] And Parnell—like Joan, like O'Connor—ignoring conventional morality, found his mate among the British. In earlier stories, such as "Guests of the Nation" and "The English Soldier," O'Connor presented English characters who, like Fortescue, insist upon being evaluated for themselves rather than for their nationality; in some later stories, including "The Custom of the Country" and "Darcy in the Land of Youth," Irish characters, frustrated, like Joan, by intolerance and narrowness at home, find to their surprise that the only liberating association is with the English.[36]

The rather enigmatic title of the play picks up the now-

---

35. "Come Gather Round Me Parnellites."

36. "The English Soldier," in *Bones of Contention* (New York, 1936); "The Custom of the Country," in *The Common Chord* (New York, 1948); "Darcy in the Land of Youth," in *Traveller's Samples* (New York, 1951.)

familiar identification of Parnell with Moses, but in fact fuses two different Biblical rocks. Before the split, Hegarty declares that their faith in Parnell's success "is founded on rock." The rock is identified with the loyalty of the Irish people to their leader. The image is derived from the New Testament, where a truly Christian life which provides a firm foundation for an individual or the Church is compared to a rock upon which a house may safely be built. It is contrasted to mere lip-service which, like a foundation of sand, provides no real security.[37] But Dr. Jackson responds to Hegarty's use of the metaphor by questioning whether Parnell's support is not, rather, like the other Biblical rock, "Moses' Rock."

The rock which is associated with Moses in the Old Testament is not, in fact, one upon which something is built, but one which he strikes with his miraculous rod while the Israelites are wandering in the desert. The rock opens and water gushes out of it, providing refreshment and salvation for the Israelites.[38] In the play this image seems ironic, since it is used, not in relation to a beneficial event, but in relation to the Party splitting. What is suggested is disaster, the failure of the firm foundation, at the same time that it is perhaps implied that there is something "miraculous" in such an unexpected event occurring. (O'Connor was fond of sardonically referring to the latest nine-days' wonder as "the greatest miracle since Moses split the rock," and this is an expression which still has some currency in Ireland.)[39]

It is certainly difficult to believe that the play sees the split, in itself, as a good thing for the Irish people, but perhaps in the long run it does have beneficial results. It enables Joan to see the men around her, especially Jer Coghlan and her father, in a truer light, and thus gives her the courage to make her break for freedom; it leads Aunt Kate and Dr. Jackson to new self-knowledge and re-opens their closed hearts, even if they are re-opened to suffering. Perhaps, then, the point is

---

37. See Matthew 7:24–27.

38. See Exodus 17, especially 6–7, also Numbers 20:6–11. The miracle of the rock bringing forth water is referred to in many other places in the Old Testament; however, relevant English translations do not use the word "split" to describe what happened to the rock. Various other terms such as "cleft" and "opened" are used.

39. This information was provided by Harriet Sheehy in conversation.

that the rock which seemed a broken foundation proves in fact to be Moses' rock, bringing renewed life and blessing.

In addition to considering a particularly fascinating set of events in Ireland's political history, *Moses' Rock*, through its choice of characters, also provides something of a cross-section of Cork society and crystallizes a particular stage in Ireland's social history. The household of the butter merchant Cady O'Leary is not unlike the kind of Cork household in which O'Connor's mother worked as a servant before her marriage. The period was, as O'Connor observed, "the great age of the butter-and-egg trade."[40] The burgeoning of the middle classes in this period is related to an urbanization process which was not, in Ireland, dependent upon industrialization to the extent that it was in many other countries. Social change is shown through the three generations of O'Leary's family: his mother, Shuvaun, is an Irish speaker with a long memory, never much at home in the urban world in which her son has established himself; Cady O'Leary has money but few pretensions to gentility, yet he has ensured that his daughter has had a convent education and he plans for her to marry a man whose status accords with it, at the same time that he fears that his sister, who has eschewed his social ambitions, will jeopardize the family's standing.

These characters mingle in the play with other representatives of the Cork world of Parnell's time. Biddy and Sorry, the women "of the lanes," passionate, quarrelsome and vital, represent a group which provided O'Connor with many vivid characters, both in his early stories and in his first novel, *The Saint and Mary Kate* (1932). Offstage, but continually making their presence felt, are the members of the band. Bands, encouraged by the Cork-based temperance leader Father Mathew, among others, provided an activity and a sense of identity for many poor men who otherwise had nothing but the pub to turn to for recreation (although bands were by no means always committed to total abstinence). Bands were a prominent feature of the political scene at the time, although O'Connor (whose father was a bandsman) more than once

---

40. *An Only Child*, p. 71.

made the point that bandsmen were chameleon-like in their ability to change political colors.[41]

But Shuvaun O'Leary, in particular, is a figure of a kind which fascinated O'Connor, especially in the 1930's and early 1940's. In these years he wrote several stories about the relationship between the older, rural, Gaelic world (whose extinction was virtually ensured by the 1890's) and the developing, English-speaking world of the growing Irish towns. Some of these stories, such as "The Majesty of the Law," "In the Train," and "The Bridal Night," are among the finest of his entire career; one of the most famous, "The Long Road to Ummera," has a central character who is based on O'Connor's own paternal grandmother, and is a more developed version of Shuvaun in *Moses' Rock*.[42]

A major cause of the depopulation of the Irish countryside in the 19th century was the potato famine of the 1840's which is vividly called up by Shuvaun's recollection of "the people dying by the roadside with the green grass in their mouths"— grass which they ate in a last desperate effort to stay alive. Those who could, emigrated; others remained behind, frequently to succumb to starvation or fever. The population of Ireland was reduced by a quarter in the course of a decade, and it was in particular the poorer, Irish-speaking districts which suffered. Survivors, like Shuvaun, moved to towns in search of a means of existence. Shuvaun provides a voice reminding her prosperous son and her convent-educated granddaughter how close they all are to the edge of the pit; the political machinations of the Coghlans and Cady O'Leary are, by contrast, shown up as petty.

41. See, for example, "The Cornet Player Who Betrayed Ireland," in the collection of the same title (Dublin, 1981).

42. "The Majesty of the Law" and "In the Train," in *Bones of Contention*. "The Bridal Night" and "The Long Road to Ummera," in *Crab Apple Jelly* (New York, 1944). See also *An Only Child*, especially Part I, for O'Connor's account of his grandmother. The character in "The Long Road to Ummera" is like Shuvaun in that she also has left her home in Ummera and has a prosperous son who does not share her memories and values, but is quite different from her in personality. The character in "The Long Road to Ummera" is called Abby Bat Heigue, a name O'Connor also used for one of the characters in his next play, *Time's Pocket*; she is different from both Shuvaun and the Abby of "The Long Road to Ummera" except for her respect for tradition. This cluster of characters provides a good illustration of the way in which O'Connor often reworked the same material many times.

The fact that grain was being exported from Ireland while people starved is one which has not been forgotten, and it was high on the list of grievances which led to demands for land reform and for political self-determination. In some cases the result was violent rebellion. One of the historical events evoked in the play is the Fenian Rising of 1867, itself a rather botched and abortive affair which had more symbolic than real significance. The term "Fenians" originally referred to Irish-Americans who had served in the American Civil War and were prepared to use their military training to free Ireland from British rule. Later the reference of the term was extended, so that it could be used loosely to mean any Irish nationalist, or, more exactly, one prepared to use violent methods.

In the middle of the 1860's the Fenians succeeded in in-filtrating British regiments stationed in Ireland—in which many of the soldiers were, of course, Irish themselves; from this position they expected to be able to overthrow the gov-ernment. It is thought that Fenian elements were particularly strong in regiments stationed in Cork. The Rising of 1867 was in fact doomed to failure because the Fenian infiltration had been discovered and largely contained before the Rising itself ever occurred.

This rising is important in *Moses' Rock* because Aunt Kate has evidently lost her Fenian lover as a result of it, and has therefore rejected both love and politics. The play does not make entirely clear what happened to Ted Fahy; it seems likely that he was a soldier, but whether he died fighting, or was captured and later executed, is not specified. That either of these fates is in fact a historically unlikely one is probably be-side the point;[43] especially in Cork, the Fenian Rising long kept a hold on the popular imagination, and O'Connor's third play, *Time's Pocket*, is about a soldier who participated in the Rising which, although it did not kill him, ruined his life and those of many others.

A few other brief evocations of earlier Irish history occur in the play, such as the suggestion that Parnell's supporters should call a "monster meeting." This was a technique devised

---

43. See Kevin B. Nowlan, "The Fenian Rising of 1867," in *The Fenian Movement*, ed. T. W. Moody (Cork, 1965), pp. 32–35.

by the most important Irish leader before Parnell, Daniel O'Connell. O'Connell succeeded in gathering literally hundreds of thousands of people at open-air meetings; this unmistakable expression of popular support for him put peaceful but strong pressure on the British government.

These references, even fleeting ones, to earlier episodes in Irish history serve to create a sense that the events presented in *Moses' Rock* are not isolated. They are part of a long continuum which does not end at the point at which the curtain comes down, any more than the story really begins at the point at which it goes up. For an Irish audience, this sense of perspective would be evoked automatically by these references, and if the audience chose to see any contemporary relevance in the comments which the play makes on Irish society and the Irish character, O'Connor, at least, would have had no objections. His two succeeding plays made his critical stance even more apparent. *Time's Pocket* attacks provincialism, narrow sexual morality, and undue clerical dominance by means of contrasting the sacrifice and suffering of the Fenian hero with the narrowness and rigidity of those on whose behalf he has acted.[44] O'Connor's last play, *The Statue's Daughter*, is the only one which carries the action up to his own time, the period of independence.[45] The play contrasts the generation which dreamed of and fought for freedom with the succeeding generation, out not for a nobler way of life but for jobs and money, whatever moral passion it has deformed into banning books and denouncing young people's courting.

Different though the plot and setting are, the analysis of the weaknesses and limitations of Irish society is essentially the same in *Moses' Rock* and in *The Statue's Daughter*. To put it another way, it is as if O'Connor, like Yeats and Joyce before him, sees all the failings he found in later Irish society there, waiting to be read, in the fall of Parnell.

---

44. *Time's Pocket* was first produced at the Abbey Theatre, 26 December 1938. It has not been published, and no complete text of it is known to exist. Incomplete texts of it may be found in the O'Connor papers, Mugar Library, Boston University, and in the National Library of Ireland.

45. *The Statue's Daughter* was first produced by the Dublin Drama League at the Gate Theatre, 8 December 1941. Published, ed. James H. Mathews, in *The Journal of Irish Literature* 4, no. 1 (January 1975), 59–117.

IV

While it is of particular interest to view *Moses' Rock* in the context of O'Connor's development as a writer, one must not lose sight of the fact that the play had two authors. Hunt describes their collaboration in the following way:

> There was no set pattern. Certainly [O'Connor] initiated the characters and plot. Then came the shaping into scenes and dialogue. This was probably mostly mine in rough draft. There followed the polishing of the dialogue which was purely Frank's. . . . In fact, there was a good deal of passing pages backwards and forwards, but, curiously enough—considering our different backgrounds—we were, on the whole, on the same wavelength.[46]

Moses' Rock was produced at the Abbey Theatre on 28 February 1938, and ran for two weeks, a standard run at the time. It has not been revived. Newspaper reviewers praised the production, particularly the acting, although the influential "Andrew E. Malone" of the *Irish Times* felt that there were weaknesses in the play's dramatic construction, notably in the fact that, of the many characters, "only five or six . . . are intimately associated with the action of the play."[47] Malone is here pointing to a problem which in fact bedevils all of O'Connor's plays: often the most memorable characters seem to have been included because they are vividly imagined in themselves, not because they are essential to the action. The three old women in *Moses' Rock*, and even to a large extent Cady O'Leary himself, are certainly not essential to the plot, whatever they contribute to the theme and the general vitality of the play.

To look at this problem in another way, O'Connor was, at this stage in his career, generally more successful at creating middle-aged and older characters than he was at presenting young, romantic figures, even though it is on these latter that the plot of *Moses' Rock* turns. Jer Coghlan, who has the makings of a villain, is more individualized than the other young

---

46. Letter to Ruth Sherry, 12 September 1981.

47. Review signed "A. E. M." (Andrew E. Malone, pseud. of Laurence Patrick Byrne), *The Irish Times*, 11 March 1938.

characters, but Hegarty, Fortescue and Joan are on the whole stock "juvenile leads," although the actress Shelah Richards clearly managed to create a lively and distinctive figure out of Joan in the Abbey production.

David Sears, in the *Irish Independent*, praised *Moses' Rock* as "sound and wise . . . searching in its analysis of national and personal emotions . . . comprehensive in its imaginative span," but, far from seeing any contemporary relevance for the play, he assumed that it shows a *fin de siècle* exhaustion in Ireland; "it was the end of an era and the race was old and sick." By contrast, he says, the audience has known "the re-vivifying spring of the Twentieth Century that was to quicken a new generation."[48] But Lia Clarke, writing for the *Irish Press*, emphasizes Joan's disillusionment and feels that "there is bitterness in this play,"[49] although she avoids any further specification of what might lie behind the bitterness.

There has been very little critical comment on any of O'Connor's plays except in the form of newspaper reviews of productions; only in recent years has any of the plays been published, and authoritative texts have been difficult or impossible to obtain. The only substantial comment on the plays is found in Roger McHugh's essay, "Frank O'Connor and the Irish Theatre,"[50] which was written before any of the plays was published and therefore devotes most of its attention to description of them rather than to critical comment. McHugh feels, however, that *Moses' Rock* is the best of O'Connor's plays,[51] and asserts that his work encouraged the generation of Irish dramatists active during World War II to write plays based upon historical material.

Present-day readers, who have had no opportunity to see the play performed, may nevertheless recognize its strengths. These include several instances of vivid, memorable characterization and dialogue which, if occasionally wooden, is at

---

48. Review signed "D. S.," 1 March 1938.

49. Review signed "L. C." [Lia Clarke = Geraldine Cummins Clarke], 1 March 1938.

50. *Eire/Ireland* 4, no. 2 (Summer 1969), 52–63.

51. This estimate is slightly modified in the brief mention made of the play in Maurice Harmon and Roger McHugh, *A History of Anglo-Irish Literature* (Dublin, 1982), p. 293.

best convincingly authentic and lively. The dialogue, in particular, connects the play with that tradition of Irish comedy which extends from Sheridan and Goldsmith through Wilde and Shaw to O'Casey and Behan. Yet the play, like much of the best modern drama, cannot be labelled simply. Its modulations from the comic to the sombre are skillfully controlled and provide it with a quality of maturity which makes it a worthy contribution to the tradition of literary treatments of Parnell and his fall.

It was in the late 1930's and the early 1940's that O'Connor acquired the reputation he held for rather a long time in Ireland—that of an iconoclastic, anti-clerical, bitter writer whose notions of morality were, at best, "continental," and who had, in effect, rejected and reviled the country of his birth. It is perhaps easy enough to believe in this image of O'Connor if one looks only at his plays, or at his 1940 novel, *Dutch Interior*, the first of several books banned by the Irish Censorship Board.[52] Certainly O'Connor's plays, including *Moses' Rock*, reflect his disenchantment with the Ireland which had emerged in place of the ideal for which he had once fought and for which many others had given or ruined their lives. Only *The Statue's Daughter* treats this issue directly in a contemporary situation; the other plays place the failings of the nation in an historical context. By this approach O'Connor was able to suggest that earlier nationalists, ignoring the evidence before their eyes, had overestimated Ireland's capacity for becoming a free and glorious nation. The ideal they fought for was something that Irish culture—"Lilliput," as he and O'Faolain were fond of calling it—would never permit to come into being. O'Connor thus implies that there was a fundamental flaw in the nationalist vision but avoids taking the unacceptable stance of attacking heroes like Joe Brady and Parnell, who were themselves capable of living up to their ideals. Perhaps it is because he does retain this respect for nationalist heroes that O'Connor's plays were never attacked for their content, as *Dutch Interior* and some of his short stories were.

But in the light of O'Connor's career as a whole, a characterization of him as bitter, disillusioned, and rejecting of Ireland seems startling. All of O'Connor's stories, plays and

---

52. *Dutch Interior* (New York, 1940).

novels are set in Ireland, and his affection for the land and its people is apparent. His later stories about priests belie the notion that he was anti-clerical; he virtually made a specialty of writing about lively, appealing young women like Joan O'Leary, almost all of whom manage to find highly suitable husbands among their countrymen. O'Connor's devotion to Ireland's history, architecture, language, and literature never waned. If, in the 1930's and 1940's, he permitted himself to raise a voice which could at times seem highly critical, he was doing no more than many other writers of his generation, like O'Faolain, Patrick Kavanagh and Denis Johnston, who had to find their own way in a world where it was no longer enough to serve Ireland by proclaiming her suppressed glories.

O'Connor felt that his own work "came out of a nationalism that had achieved its result and was ready to look at everyday things with a new respect." As he observed himself, one of his own contributions to the development of the new Irish literature was his depiction of "the Irish middleclass Catholic way of life with its virtues and its faults without any of the picturesqueness of earlier Irish writing . . . of romantics acting on a supercharged nationalism."[53] This all-but-forgotten play, *Moses' Rock*, gives a new dimension to our understanding of his achievement.

A NOTE ON THE TEXT

The only text of *Moses' Rock* which is at present known to exist is one in the possession of O'Connor's family; however, this text lacks an ending. For purposes of this edition, Hugh Hunt has reconstructed the ending of the play.

A few obvious spelling errors have been silently corrected, but no attempt has been made to normalize the text where it indicates pronunciation by spelling. Words in the Irish language are italicized, but not words of Irish derivation which have become part of the English dialect of Ireland.

---

53. "Foreword," *Stories by Frank O'Connor*, vii–viii.

BIBLIOGRAPHY

This bibliography is divided into two sections. The first lists works by O'Connor and/or Hunt which are relevant to their activities at the Abbey Theatre; it includes O'Connor's autobiographical writings and his later critical writings about drama and the theatre. The second section gives a brief overview of relevant secondary material about the Abbey Theatre, about O'Connor's work, and about Parnell.

Primary

Hunt, Hugh *The Abbey: Ireland's National Theatre 1904–1979* (Dublin: Gill and Macmillan; New York: Columbia University Press, 1979).

In the Train. A Drama in One Act. Adapted from a Short Story by Frank O'Connor (New York: Samuel French, 1973).

O'Connor, Frank *The Art of the Theatre* (Dublin: Fridberg, 1947).

The Backward Look: A Survey of Irish Literature (London, Melbourne, Toronto: Macmillan, 1967); *A Short History of Irish Literature: A Backward Look* (New York: Putnam's, 1967).

"In the Train," in Sylvan Barnet, Morton Berman, and

William Burto (eds.) *The Genius of the Irish Theatre* (New York: New American Library, 1960).

My Father's Son (Dublin: Gill and Macmillan, 1968; New York: Knopf, 1969).

An Only Child (London: Macmillan: New York: Knopf, 1961).

The Road to Stratford (London: Methuen, 1948).

Shakespeare's Progress (Cleveland, Ohio: World Publishing Co., 1960; New York: Collier Books, 1961).

The Statue's Daughter in *Journal of Irish Literature* Vol. 4 no. 1 (January 1975), 59–117.

O'Connor, Frank and Hunt, Hugh *The Invincibles* ([Newark, Del.:] Proscenium Press, 1980).

Secondary

Bew, Paul *C. S. Parnell* (Dublin: Gill and Macmillan, 1980).

Hogan, Robert and O'Neill, Michael J. (eds.) *Joseph Holloway's Irish Theatre*, Vol. 2 1932–1937 (Dixon, California: Proscenium Press, 1969); Vol. 3 1938–1944 (Dixon, California: Proscenium Press, 1970).

Kavanagh, Peter *The Story of the Abbey Theatre* (New York: Devin-Adair, 1950).

Lyons, F. S. L. *Charles Stewart Parnell* (London: Collins, 1977). "The Parnell Theme in Literature" in Andrew Carpenter (ed.) *Place, Personality and the Irish Writer, Irish Literary Studies* I (Gerrards Cross, Bucks.: Colin Smythe; New York: Harper and Row, 1977).

Larkin, Emmet *The Roman Catholic Church in Ireland and the Fall of Parnell 1888–1891* (Chapel Hill: University of North Carolina Press; Liverpool: Liverpool University Press, 1979).

McHugh, Roger "Frank O'Connor and the Irish Theatre" *Eire/Ireland* Vol. 4 no. 2 (Summer, 1969), 52–63.

Sheehy, Maurice (ed.) *Michael/Frank* (London: Macmillan; Dublin: Gill and Macmillan; New York: Knopf, 1969).

MOSES' ROCK

A play in three acts
by
FRANK O'CONNOR
and
HUGH HUNT

Moses' Rock was produced at the Abbey Theatre by Hugh Hunt, 28 February 1938, in a setting designed by Tanya Moiseiwitsch and with the following cast:

CADY O'LEARY (a merchant)	W. O'Gorman
KATE O'LEARY (his sister)	Ann Clery
JOAN O'LEARY (his daughter)	Shelah Richards
SHUVAUN O'LEARY (his mother)	Shela Ward
NED HEGARTY (a poet)	Cyril Cusack
JER COGHLAN (a lawyer)	Fred Johnson
LIEUTENANT GRANT FORTESCUE	P. H. Considine
DR. CORNEY JACKSON	Liam Redmond
BIDDY LALLY	Christine Hayden
SORRY O'SULLIVAN	Evelyn MacNeice
NELLY, a maid	Gertrude Quinn

Scene—*A room off the dining-room of O'Leary's house in Cork.*

ACT ONE

*[A room off the dining-room in O'Leary's house in December 1890.
The room is well furnished in the fashion of the day. Through a big
window we can see the lights of other houses on the opposite side of
the road, for it is night and the lamps in the room are lit. There are
two doors, one leading to the dining-room and one to the rest of the
house. When the curtain rises three old women are grouped round a
table sewing; two of them, BIDDY and SORRY, wear shawls and
have evidently come in for the evening. BIDDY is a stout, buxom
woman, whilst SORRY is a thin pale ghost of a creature. SHU-
VAUN is the oldest of the three and is, perhaps, a little weak in
the head. From the dining-room comes the sound of laughter and the
voices of a few men singing "The Felons of our Land", at the con-
clusion of which the door from the dining-room opens and NELLIE,
the maid, comes in.]*

    NELLIE Are ye all right?
    SHUVAUN What are they doing now?
    NELLIE They're at the desert.[1]
    SHUVAUN And what's that?

---

1. *the desert.* i.e., dessert.

NELLIE Ah, you wouldn't understand. I'm going down for the wine before they'll begin on the toasts.

SHUVAUN Musha,[2] and is it wine he's giving them. I thought he'd give them whiskey. I suppose the poor boy can't afford it.

NELLIE Stop there now, leave ye, till ye'll hear the speeches. *[Exits door up.]*
[Laughter off.]

BIDDY Speeches! Did you hear that, Shuvaun O'Leary? Did you ever think the day would come that a son of yours would be entertaining like that?

SHUVAUN I did not, Biddy, I did not, *a stor.*[3] There's great changes.

SORRY Ah, great changes, great changes! I hope they're all for the best.

BIDDY *[truculently]* And why wouldn't they?

SORRY Ah, I don't know, Biddy, I don't know. I'm only saying I hope they are.

BIDDY Maybe 'tisn't for the best that Shuvaun O'Leary that drove the little vegeatable[4] cart around this locality is sitting at her ease in the finest house in it and her son drinking wine with the best in the land.

SORRY I don't know I'm sure, Biddy, but I hope so, I hope so. We can be sure of nothing only our last end and little we'll bring with us when that time comes.

BIDDY Ah, botheration to you and your ullagoning![5] Haven't your own son a fine public house, him that had nothing but an old leaky thatch over him the time he was in Carrignagoshel?

SORRY Ah, now, 'tisn't a bad pub, praise be to God! but 'tisn't a good one either, and at home in Carrignagoshel we had a fine house and good neighbours. I often said it, I was sorry I came.

BIDDY Ah, musha, 'twouldn't be like you not to have

---

2. *Musha,* An exclamation, a disguised form of the name of Mary.

3. *a stor.* Irish = my treasure. A frequently used endearment. Spelling is not consistent in the MS., which here gives an anglicized spelling, *asthore.*

4. *vegeatable* i.e., vegetable, spelled to indicate pronunciation.

5. *ullagoning!* Complaining. From Irish *olagón* = a lament or dirge.

the poor mouth!⁶ Shuvaun will bear me out. You saw the famine, Shuvaun?

SHUVAUN I did, *a laogh liom,*⁷ I did.

BIDDY You saw the people dying by the roadside with the green grass in their mouth?

SHUVAUN Why do you remember me of it, *a stor*? I did so, I did.

BIDDY And here's your son after buying out the best house in Cork City. Tell me, Shuvaun, have you two more years in you?

SHUVAUN The day we left Ummera, Cady was only a boy of nine; Kate was six. I took them to their father's grave and I made them promise to bring me there when my time was up. The street was empty, Biddy, *a chroi 'stigh.*⁸ Forty fine houses and not a fire in one of them. There wasn't a soul alive in Ummera only the blind woman that came every day and sat in the sun outside the weaver's house. "Bride," says I, "Bride, don't you remember me, don't you remember Shuvaun Hamish Owen that used to play about your floor," and she looked at me with her sightless eyes and says she, "There is no child laughed here in the memory of man."

BIDDY I asked have you two more years in you?

SHUVAUN What's that? I have not, *a chumann.*⁹ With the rheumatics and the windy pains I haven't much longer to live.

BIDDY Live two years more then and you'll see those inside ruling the land and the ones of the spite that won't have a roof to their heads.

SORRY So they're saying, so they're saying, but I wouldn't be certain of anything in this world.

[NELLIE *comes in carrying a bottle and a few glasses.*]

BIDDY Will I open the door for you, Nellie?

NELLIE Thank you, Biddy, leave it open a crack now and you'll hear the better. [*She goes out into the dining-room.*]

---

6. *to have the poor mouth!* To insist habitually that you are poor or unfortunate when you really aren't.

7. *a laogh liom,* Irish = my own darling (literally, my bright calf). An endearment used by women to children.

8. *a chroi 'stigh.* Irish = my heart of hearts, my darling.

9. *a chumann.* Irish = my dear, my friend.

BIDDY [at the dining-room door] Settle yourself on this side, Shuvaun, and you'll see the great company at your ease.

SHUVAUN I'll stay where I am, I can't see that far.

SORRY [rising and going over to BIDDY] What is it? Let me see.

BIDDY Whisht! Whisht![10] or they'll hear you; go back and be quiet, woman.

SORRY [disconsolately returning to her place] Tell us so, can't you?

BIDDY There's only the one woman in it.

SHUVAUN Is it fine the company looks, a stor?

BIDDY Solid silver and Waterford glass! 'Twould take the sight out of your eyes.[11]

SORRY To think that a bare-footed boy from Carrignagoshel owns it all!

BIDDY And then ye'll say 'tisn't for the better. Ah, the gentry of Cork know whether 'tis for the better or not, Sorry Sullivan. 'Tis they'll be peeping out from under their blinds this night. But the time is past when they could trample on us. [Almost dancing with excitement.] 'Tis past, 'tis past. We can walk the streets of Cork without "by your leave" to the best of them.

SHUVAUN Tell me what way is Joan, Biddy?

BIDDY Shining she is. Like a lady. Ah, well you may be proud of a granddaughter the like of her. The way the young men are leaning up to her, trying to look her in her face.

SHUVAUN Who are they at all, Biddy?

BIDDY Ned Hegarty and Jer Coghlan, old Dan's son, the lawyer. There's one each side of her. A lovely picture they make, God bless and spare them.

SHUVAUN Is that one of the Hegartys of Crisslaugh, Biddy?

BIDDY Not at all, not at all! 'Tis the writing fellow that done the six months and was left out of gaol today, the one Cady is giving the dinner for. His mother had the little huxter's shop[12] in Douglas Street.

---

10. *Whisht! Whisht!* Hush, be quiet!

11. *'Twould take the sight out of your eyes.* It would dazzle you.

12. *huxter's shop* Small grocery shop.

SHUVAUN Sure, I gets mixed, Biddy. I thought 'twas Jer Coghlan 'twas after coming out of gaol.

BIDDY No, no. Jer defended him at the trial—don't you remember? He flung his papers in the judge's face. Himself and Hegarty are friends since the time they were children.

SHUVAUN And which of them is going to marry our Joan?

BIDDY I didn't hear either of them was to marry her, but by the look of it, I wouldn't say they'd have much objection.

SHUVAUN Maybe I'm wrong, maybe I'm wrong. No one tells me anything. I must ask me daughter. Where's Kate? Is she inside there too?

BIDDY Don't you know well she's not inside, but down in the kitchen sulking. She come up to ready the dinner for Cady but the devil himself wouldn't make her sit at his table.

SHUVAUN Ah, poor girl, 'twas the disappointment. She was very great with a boy[13] one time.

BIDDY There's Cady getting up. Keep quiet now, the pair of ye. He's going to speak.

SHUVAUN Have he drink taken, Biddy? 'Tis an old fault of his.

BIDDY He's holding on to the table. He have a drop in sure enough. Listen!

. *[Applause.]*

O'LEARY *[off]* Mr. Hegarty, my friends, my old friends. I find it hard to say the pleasure 'tis to me tonight to have ye under my roof. As ye know, 'tis the first dinner party I have given in this house, but I hope 'twon't be the last. *[Applause.]* But I'll say this; however many I give there'll be none that'll be as great a satisfaction as this one, to welcome back to liberty as fine a young man as ever lost it for the sake of Ireland. *[Applause.]* I mean, Mr. Ned Hegarty, the most brilliant of our young patriots. *[More applause.]* I'm not going to make a long speech; I'm sorry to say I haven't the gift; in my young days the education wasn't going[14] like it is now; but I ask ye to drink to the health of Mr. Ned Hegarty who will I hope be one of the shining lights of our new Parliament and with

---

13. *She was very great with a boy* She was keeping steady company.

14. *the education wasn't going* Education wasn't freely available.

his name I join the name of our great and glorious leader, Charles Stewart Parnell, the uncrowned king *[his voice is drowned in uproarious applause]* who will not long, I hope, be without his crown.

SHUVAUN What is it all about, Biddy? I can't hear but a few words.

BIDDY Parnell he's talking about. The uncrowned king who will not long be without his crown. God bless you, Cady Leary, and you too, Joan, me handsome girl. Look at her now, and her eyes shining. She's raising her glass to young Hegarty. A fine pair they'd make.

SORRY Whisper now, Shuvaun, I suppose Cady will be giving a tidy fortune with Joan?

SHUVAUN Ah, where would he get it, the poor boy? He have great expenses. No one knows the mint of money he spent on educating her.

BIDDY Whisht, whisht, can't ye? 'Tis young Hegarty. He's going to reply. He looks like a king, head up, hands behind his back.

[Applause.]

HEGARTY *[off]* Mr. O'Leary, and you my friends and colleagues. I thank you from the bottom of my heart. You and I have shared many things, gratification and disappointment, hope and fear in the pursuit of the ideal which is forever before our eyes, the liberation of our country. *[Applause.]* In many trials we have been sustained by one secure conviction; our faith is founded on rock.[15] *[Applause.]* Against that rock, the force, the fraud of our enemies may break in vain. Within two years we shall have achieved our objective. Perhaps it may come even sooner. You know that in London at this moment our chief, our hero, is fighting his greatest battle. Despite the calumny and odious slander of a hostile press, despite the painful proceedings of a divorce court, the Irish nation through its representatives has affirmed its faith in Mr. Parnell by electing him once more to the leadership of the party. . . .

[The door from the passage opens and KATE O'LEARY comes in. She is a tall, proud woman who has reached middle age.]

KATE Shut that door!

---

15. *our faith is founded on rock.* See Matthew 7:24–27, where firm faith is compared with a house built on a rock, while weak faith is compared with a house built upon sand.

[BIDDY does so and HEGARTY's voice stops.]

KATE   What are you doing up here in the cold, Mother?

SHUVAUN   Listening to the speeches I was, Kate *a ghradh gheal*.[16]

KATE   More fool you! Come on now.

SHUVAUN   Cady spoke. You should have heard him. Ah, musha, it brought it all back, the old times, when we'd be waiting up for the police. Kate, I was trying to think. What was the name of the boy that used to be always at the house? *[Pause. KATE crosses to window, arranges curtains.]* The tall dark boy?

BIDDY   Whisht, woman, whisht!

SHUVAUN   Why would I whisht? Sure, he was very great with Kate. There was only the breath of life between them.[17]

BIDDY   Can't you see you're upsetting her?

SHUVAUN   Kate! What is it, child? I forgot—my head goes. Sure, he's dead.

[Applause.]

KATE   *[turns]* And more shame for you, Biddy Donoghue, to be dragging her up to listen to that ramaish.[18]

BIDDY   Now, Kate, 'tis true, every word of it.

KATE   Ramaish!

BIDDY   You'll see!

KATE   Oh, I'll see, never fear. The day the Hegartys and the Coghlans free Ireland, with their speech-making, I'll walk to Croagh Patrick[19] in my bare feet doing penance.

BIDDY   Ah, Kate, why will you be so bitter? We know well your heart was with the Fenians, but aren't the best of them behind the chief today?

KATE   Ay, behind a damned adulterer.

BIDDY   Don't anger me now, Kate.

KATE   A damned adulterer and his English fancy-woman!

---

16. *a gradh gheal.*   Irish = sweetheart, dearly beloved.

17. *There was only the breath of life between them.*   Their hearts beat as one, they were as close as they could be.

18. *ramaish.*   Nonsense, twaddle. From Irish *raméis* = nonsensical talk.

19. *Croagh Patrick*   A mountain in Co. Mayo which is a place of pilgrimage. As an act of devotion, people often climb it barefoot.

BIDDY [*flaring up*] Ah, get out of me sight. 'Twas an ease to Ted Fahy the day he died not to have to live with the likes of you.

KATE   Don't mention his name.

BIDDY   Go on, you sour ould thing! You're black from the heart out.[20]

KATE   Come on, Mother.

SHUVAUN   What are ye fighting about? 'Twas my fault. Sure, why do ye mind me? I don't know what I do be saying. [*Exits with* KATE.]

BIDDY   Isn't she a bitter vindictive ould thing. Oh, God forgive me, what did I say to her?

SORRY   She's that black she'll hate you till the day she die.

BIDDY   Oh, God, sure I never meant it.

SORRY   There you are! I do be always telling you. Too high up in yourself you are always, and there never was a high heart but the Lord lowered it.

BIDDY   Musha, is it under the bushes you'd have us hide? 'Tis her own fault.

[*The dining-room door opens and* JOAN O'LEARY *comes in. She is in evening dress, a handsome girl of eighteen.*]

JOAN   What's happening in here?

BIDDY   Nothing, *stor*, nothing. We were listening to the speeches.

JOAN   I heard Aunt Kate raising her voice to you.

BIDDY   Ah, 'twas just a little argument. Lucky you are, child, she never took it into her head to come and live with ye.

JOAN   What did she say?

BIDDY   Ah, she was against us on account of listening to Mr. Hegarty speaking.

JOAN   The bitter old thing!

BIDDY   The bitter old thing! That's what I say. And he the finest young man that walks Cork.

JOAN   Do you think so, Biddy?

BIDDY   Erra,[21] do I think so? Ah, Joan, a happy girl I'd think you if you ever got the likes of him for a husband.

---

20. *black from the heart out.*   Sour, bad-tempered, bitter.

21. *Erra,*   Yes, sure. Also occurs as "Yerrah". Another exclamation derived from the name of Mary.

JOAN Well, now, maybe I might.

BIDDY Is that the way of it? Ah, the blessings of God and His Blessed Mother on you, child.

[NELLIE *comes in from the dining-room.*]

NELLIE Are ye there yet? Come on now, down with ye, down with ye to the kitchen. I'll make a cup of tea for ye when the table is cleared.

SORRY Nellie, if there's e'er a little sup over. . . .

NELLIE Downstairs with ye! Hurry up! [BIDDY *and* SORRY *exit.*] I'm kilt with work. I'll be after you in two minutes. Lookit, Miss Joan, what made you pick on tonight of all nights?

JOAN What is it, Nellie?

NELLIE Now, what do you think? The English officer is below wanting to see you.

JOAN How dare he come here? Tell him to go away.

NELLIE Sure, I did but he's mad. I stepped down for the wine and he was in the kitchen, straight from the barracks he's come in full uniform.

JOAN My God, he'll be seen. Where is he now?

NELLIE In the linen cupboard. If your father catches him, I'm sacked. Musha, Joan, what came over you? As if there weren't boys enough walking Cork?

JOAN You'll have to keep him there till the dining-room is clear. Do you hear me?

NELLIE Oh, I hear you. I'll give him a glass of whiskey. But look, Joan, don't keep me long for the love of God. The band is below.

JOAN What band?

NELLIE Your father sent for the band to serenade Ned Hegarty and they're below, thirty of them, drinking porter all over the place. We'll be caught as sure as fortune.

JOAN Start clearing up in the dining-room the way you'll hurry them out. I'll go downstairs till they're all below. Quick!

[*They both rush out. After a while the door opens and HE-GARTY and COGHLAN come in. They are both under thirty, but COGHLAN looks older than HEGARTY.*]

HEGARTY [*closing the door behind him as well as the door onto the landing*] I want a few words with you, Jer.

COGHLAN What is it?

HEGARTY   I saw your sister for a few minutes today.

COGHLAN   Oh!

HEGARTY   She told me something I hadn't suspected.

COGHLAN   Oh! And what was that?

HEGARTY   You'll forgive me, Jer?

COGHLAN   Do you think there's anything you couldn't say to me?

HEGARTY   I wonder if everyone's as blind as I am? It seems incredible that one can care deeply for somebody, meet them every day for years, discuss everything on heaven and earth with them, and not realise the most obvious thing about them.

COGHLAN   I don't know what you're talking about.

HEGARTY   You knew I was in love with Joan.

COGHLAN   Of course I did. You're not opaque.

HEGARTY   Will you believe me when I say that until today it never crossed my mind, never in my wildest dreams, that you felt the same way about her. Never until your sister told me today when I went to tea in the convent.

COGHLAN   You surely don't believe her?

HEGARTY   Of course I do.

COGHLAN   Really, really! This is maddening. Will you believe me now when I say it's all nonsense.

HEGARTY   No.

COGHLAN   I may have mentioned something of the kind to her but it was only in passing. I wasn't serious.

HEGARTY   Of course you were serious. Far more serious than I have been. You did the thing I should have done. You realised that someone else was concerned and concealed your real feelings. Oh, Jer, will you ever forgive me?

COGHLAN   But I tell you there's nothing to forgive.

HEGARTY   Oh, of course there is. I had made up my mind to ask Joan to marry me this very night. Providence saved me.

COGHLAN   What nonsense! If you've made up your mind then you certainly must ask her.

HEGARTY   *[explosively]* No!

COGHLAN   But you must. Do you think I can accept such sacrifices from you?

HEGARTY   Do you think I can accept such sacrifices from you, a man who has done what you've done for the past year or two? No, Jer. Whatever happens, Joan mustn't come between you and me. We'll both try to forget it.

COGHLAN   Oh, Quixote, Quixote![22]

HEGARTY   I have no reason to think she cares for me.

COGHLAN   No? You think she went every day to the gaol for the sake of the exercise. I tell you I've seen her. You'll propose to her this very night, or I'll propose for you.

HEGARTY   And lose my best friend?

COGHLAN   I'll still be your friend.

HEGARTY   A few months won't make any difference.

COGHLAN   You know very little about women if you think that.

HEGARTY   Joan is different. Besides, you know what I feel. I believe the present crisis is the last. When this has been surmounted the English will cave in. I shouldn't be surprised if within six months we have Home Rule. Then everything will be different. We shall all know our own minds better. At present we are living under abnormal conditions. Who knows? Perhaps I may be the very first to change.

COGHLAN   Oh Ned, Ned, what am I to do with you? You're so utterly guileless.

HEGARTY   We won't either of us think about it again for a few months. Is that agreed?

COGHLAN   All right, Ned, if that makes your mind easier. *[They shake hands.]*

[CADY O'LEARY and DR. JACKSON come in from the dining-room. O'LEARY is a shrewd business man whose perpetual desire to be in on the right side of the fence is only tempered by his fear of what his friends will think of him. JACKSON is approaching fifty; he has an autocratic "Old World" manner, and delights in stepping outside life and adopting the role of an observer.]

O'LEARY   *[a bit squiffy[23]]* I hope we're not intruding.

COGHLAN   No, no, come in.

O'LEARY   I'm having an argument, a very serious argument with me old friend Corney about your speech, Ned. *[Turns to cupboard and takes out whiskey.]*

---

22. *Quixote!*   Miguel de Cervantes' *Don Quixote* is the story of a romantic man who has lost contact with reality.

23. *squiffy*   Tipsy, drunk.

COGHLAN   'Twouldn't be the doctor if he hadn't some queer notion. How are the apes, doctor?

JACKSON   The apes at the moment are in abeyance but they won't be so long. Don't fret.

COGHLAN   I declare to God, you're a contradiction in terms, doctor. Here you are, straight out of the eighteenth century and you swallow holus, bolus,[24] the biggest nonsense of all time and believe that men are descended from apes.

HEGARTY   Ah, well, we can forgive the doctor his little weakness, but I'd like to know why you disagree with my speech, doctor.

JACKSON   Ah, never mind me. As Coghlan says, I'm an anachronism. Talk on, talk on. I like listening. Such youth, such eloquence, such enthusiasm!

HEGARTY   Now you're being sarcastic.

JACKSON   Not I. I revel in it. You make me feel so old and wise.

COGHLAN   A whig, that's what you are. A damned whig.[25]

JACKSON   Indulge an old man in his simple pleasures. Yes, I am a bit of a whig.

COGHLAN   A whig and a Darwinist. It's a contradiction in terms.

O'LEARY   I don't know what in hell are ye talking about, but the doctor says the Party will throw Parnell over.

JACKSON   He says nothing of the sort, Cady. He says he wouldn't be a bit surprised if they did.

HEGARTY   You really believe that possible, doctor?

JACKSON   Seriously, I do.

HEGARTY   But, it's nonsense. They're not fools. We have everything in our hands; a strong leader, a universal confidence, a united country. You can feel it in the air; it's like the way you can smell the dawn before it comes.

JACKSON   A little too bright, a little too sudden.

---

24. *swallow holus, bolus.*   Swallow whole, accept gullibly.

25. *whig.*   The term was originally applied to anti-Royalist, anti-episcopal Scottish Presbyterians. Later it was used to refer to those of a liberal political tendency. In a general sense the term suggests someone who questions existing systems and beliefs. Coghlan's remark, a few lines below, to the effect that being a whig is inconsistent with being a Darwinist, presumably implies that to accept Darwin's theories requires naive gullibility rather than the skeptical frame of mind usually associated with whigs.

COGHLAN But it isn't sudden. For years we've been working for it. We've disciplined the people. Nothing on heaven or earth could stop them now. We've fought the landlords and beaten them to their knees. We've fought the military, we've fought the police. We have a people like a rock.

JACKSON Moses' Rock. I doubt that united people of yours, Coghlan. They've never been tested and the test must come.

HEGARTY Every man in Ireland will stand behind Parnell.

JACKSON I wonder, I wonder.

O'LEARY Oh God, 'tis useless talking to you. Here, have a drink. 'Twill put some bounce into you.

JACKSON No, I must go down and have a look at your mother. I daren't face Kate with the sign of drink on me.

O'LEARY Is it her? Sure, she's used to it. That shop of hers is always full of the worst boozers in Cork.

JACKSON That's a grand woman, Cady. You could do worse than have her to keep house for you.

O'LEARY She's a sour old maid. She'd drive me to drink in a week.

JACKSON 'Twould be more remarkable if she kept you off it that long.

O'LEARY Well, I'm having another now, Kate or no Kate. I want a few words with Ned here.

JACKSON Come, Coghlan. We'll talk to the old lady about her windy pains.

COGHLAN Yes, we can tell her that the boss is taking the treatment for her. [*They go out by the door leading to the rest of the house.*]

O'LEARY Well now, what the devil did he mean by that?

HEGARTY You had something to say to me, Mr. O'Leary?

O'LEARY Those Coghlans are very ignorant. Always making jokes about you.

HEGARTY Ah, he didn't mean it.

O'LEARY Well, now, let me see, Ned. I wanted to speak to you. The devil fly away with him, he has had me all upset. "Taking the treatment" indeed!

HEGARTY Never mind that just at present.

O'LEARY   I'll make a mess of it. I know I will. Joan will never let me hear the end of it.

HEGARTY   The end of what, Mr. O'Leary?

O'LEARY   Half the troubles of this country are caused by people being funny at the wrong time. Another drop of whiskey in my glass, Ned, if you please.

HEGARTY   There you are. And now what is it?

O'LEARY   Ned, boy, 'tisn't the couple of drinks—

HEGARTY   No, of course, certainly not.

O'LEARY   You know I feel towards you like a father.

HEGARTY   I know that, sir. You've always been kindness itself.

O'LEARY   So now that you're out of gaol and after landing the good job you were after it might be no harm if we talked about a certain little matter we were discussing the day before you were tried.

HEGARTY   I remember, Mr. O'Leary. I'm not likely to forget.

O'LEARY   I was just wondering were you still of the same mind?

HEGARTY   When you know me better you'll know that I never change.

O'LEARY   Just so, just so. You're like myself. Well, on that occasion you asked permission to pay attention to my daughter and I told you I'd be delighted. Well, of course, the gaol put a stop to that, but I didn't forget it. I took the liberty of mentioning the matter to Joan and she, I'm glad to say, was as pleased as I was.

HEGARTY   Is that so, Mr. O'Leary?

O'LEARY   It is so. There's no one in the wide world she thinks more of than yourself and as you know she's of a very loving disposition. Now, I'm not the man I was. I'm getting old. One of these days I'll be joining my poor Julia in Caherlag.[26] Since you spoke to me I was thinking a lot about it and considering that you're off to Dublin tomorrow, I was thinking if you're still of the same mind, there's no reason we wouldn't have something definite settled tonight.

HEGARTY   Tonight? Oh, yes. I see what you mean.

O'LEARY   Ye won't be badly off. Anything I have will

---

26. *Caherlag.* The place where Julia is buried. The name appears to be imaginary.

come to her, sooner or later, and if some of it comes sooner
so much the better.

HEGARTY   Money doesn't worry me.

O'LEARY   A wife will soon cure you of that.

HEGARTY   I doubt if anyone will cure me.

O'LEARY   Well, we'll see. But now, what do you say?
We'll never have a better chance of announcing it?

HEGARTY   Mr. O'Leary, I'm sorry, but it's impossible.

O'LEARY   Impossible? And for why?

HEGARTY   Not for some time at any rate. I'm in a very
difficult position.

O'LEARY   But what is there to stop you? There isn't another girl, surely?

HEGARTY   Certainly not. There never has been. There
never will be.

O'LEARY   But then, I can't see—

HEGARTY   Mr. O'Leary, this is a matter that concerns
my best friend. He's in love with Joan. I only discovered it
today by accident. I couldn't become engaged to Joan, at least
until he's had a chance of finding out his own mind. It may
be only a fancy of his. Give him a few months, Mr. O'Leary.
If Joan and I were to become engaged now he might go on
all his life thinking I had cheated him.

O'LEARY   But who is it? I didn't know there was anyone
else?

HEGARTY   Coghlan, Jer Coghlan.

O'LEARY   Dan Coghlan's boy?

HEGARTY   Yes.

O'LEARY   But that's impossible. I wouldn't allow it. I
couldn't think of such a match. Joan isn't going to marry a
Coghlan if he was the last man in the world.

HEGARTY   Even so, Mr. O'Leary, for his own sake, for
the sake of our friendship. That means a great deal to me.

O'LEARY   Oh, now, that's all very well. But the girl's
mind is made up. 'Tis you she wants, not Jer Coghlan, and
'twon't be very pleasant to know she's being put off to oblige
him.

HEGARTY   Mr. O'Leary, I hope you won't mention anything about this to her.

O'LEARY   Well, someone's got to explain to the girl.
Every day, wet or fine, up to the gaol; not a thought in her

head from morning to night only you. Oh, I don't understand all this fine talk, Mr. Hegarty; 'tis a bit beyond me.

HEGARTY Leave me to do the explaining. I know I can make Joan understand.

O'LEARY Maybe you can, maybe you can, but 'tis a great disappointment.

[JOAN comes in.]

JOAN Look, are you going to stay there all night? They're looking for ye downstairs.

O'LEARY Yes, I'd better be going. This young gentleman has some explaining to do.

JOAN Explaining?

HEGARTY Not now, Mr. O'Leary. Tomorrow. My train doesn't go till the afternoon.

O'LEARY What's wrong with now? Didn't you say you'd do the job?

JOAN What's all this about? Ye look vexed, the pair of ye.

HEGARTY Tomorrow, Joan. It's a long and rather delicate story.

O'LEARY All right, all right. I can see you're going to leave it to me.

HEGARTY Mr. O'Leary, this is neither the time nor the place for explaining. I don't want to embarrass Joan. I don't want to embarrass Mr. Coghlan.

JOAN What's the mystery? What's this about Mr. Coghlan?

O'LEARY All right, young man, clear out. I'll do me duty as a father. Clear out if you won't stand by your words.

HEGARTY I'm thinking of Joan, Mr. O'Leary.

O'LEARY I thought you said you were thinking of Coghlan. Go on now. Ah, if my poor Julia was alive I wouldn't be the way I am.

HEGARTY Joan, your father isn't himself tonight. I'll be up in the morning, about eleven.

JOAN Very well, Ned, but I'm sure I don't know what 'tis all about.

[HEGARTY exits.]

Well? Oh, you needn't tell me. You made a mess of it, I know.

O'LEARY Oh, let me alone. The whole world is gone mad—I must get a little press[27] for that corner.

JOAN What is it?

O'LEARY Oh, some rigmarole or other. The gaol is after driving him dotty. Imagine letting himself be turned over by a Coghlan.

JOAN What's that?

O'LEARY Dan Coghlan's Jer. He wants to marry you as well.

JOAN And he never let on. There's cuteness for you.

O'LEARY Too cute for my liking. There's something deep about this. A wonder Dan Coghlan never mentioned it to me himself. There's something deep, there's something very like a plot in this. I wish I could see my way in it.

JOAN If you go on with that whiskey, you won't see anything at all. Go on up now.

O'LEARY I'll have to think it out. I'll have to think it all out, this blessed night. Ah, if your poor mother was alive she wouldn't be long disentangling it for me. That was a woman that had a mind like a corkscrew.

[O'LEARY goes. JEAN hurries to the dining-room door, calls "Nellie!" and then carefully shuts the other door. NELLIE comes in.]

NELLIE Are they all downstairs?

JOAN Yes. Where is he?

NELLIE Still in the linen cupboard.

JOAN Bring him up, Nellie.

NELLIE God grant I'm not seen.

[NELLIE exits. After a moment's interval the door opens quietly and LIEUTENANT FORTESCUE steals in and closes it just as quietly behind him.]

JOAN Grant! How dare you?

FORTESCUE I couldn't help it.

JOAN You might be seen.

FORTESCUE I had to see you. I waited all the morning in the Mardyke.[28] Why didn't you come, Joan?

JOAN I couldn't.

FORTESCUE And you didn't send me word?

---

27. *press* Cupboard.

28. *the Mardyke.* A street in Cork where fashionable people went walking.

JOAN   I didn't know till 'twas too late.

FORTESCUE   It isn't anything you heard? You've nothing against me, have you?

JOAN   No, nothing.

FORTESCUE   And you won't do this to me again?

JOAN   Grant, I can't see you again. You mustn't come here again. I don't know what I've been doing to meet you at all, it's got to stop. My father would turn me out of the house if he knew I was meeting you.

FORTESCUE   I'd look after you.

JOAN   But I don't want to be looked after. I don't want to break my father's heart.

FORTESCUE   We'd get married and after a time he'd get used to the idea. They all do.

JOAN   Grant, I'd never marry anybody without father's consent. I'd have no luck afterwards.

FORTESCUE   We could leave here tomorrow and be married in London.

JOAN   I haven't the courage, Grant—that's all about it.[29]

FORTESCUE   And you're going to marry some wretched little shopkeeper, and spend the rest of your days in this dull hole? Joan, do you know what you're doing?

JOAN   It isn't a dull hole. This is the finest city in Ireland.

FORTESCUE   I know, I know, but that's not saying much. You used to say you wanted to go abroad. You haven't changed, have you?

JOAN   I don't know.

FORTESCUE   Marry me, and we'll go away together, anywhere you like. We'll go to Venice for our honeymoon and after that you can tell me about the charms of Cork, if you've the nerve!

JOAN   You know, don't you, that Cork has been called the Venice of Ireland?

FORTESCUE   Well, nobody has ever called Venice the Cork of Italy, thank God. Joan, don't talk nonsense. We'll clear out of this country for ever. You're just as tired of all these stupid people as I am.

JOAN   They're not stupid. Ned Hegarty is one of the finest intellects in the world.

---

29. *that's all about it.*   That's all there is to it, there's nothing to discuss.

FORTESCUE Who's he?

JOAN The man your gaolers released from prison today. Grant, don't you understand! That's what makes it so impossible. I can't go on meeting you like this. Think what Ned would say if he knew that I was friendly with one of the men who put him in prison.

FORTESCUE I didn't put him in prison.

JOAN No, but your country did.

FORTESCUE Well he probably damned well deserved it. And if you want me to fly into a passion of jealousy over some blinking little home-ruler, you can try again. I suppose you are contemplating marrying him?

JOAN Perhaps.

FORTESCUE Don't be a little fool. I care more for you than twenty Hegartys, and one of these days you'll find that out. Joan, my dear, don't run away from the one thing that is staring you in the face. You must continue to meet me.

JOAN I can't. It isn't that I don't want to, but I shan't be able to manage it now.

FORTESCUE You did it before.

JOAN Yes, but I'd an excuse. They thought I was only going to the gaol to enquire for Ned. Of course I was too. But now he's out of gaol I can't do it any more. That's why I didn't turn up today.

FORTESCUE Meet me tomorrow. Make some excuse. I can't talk here. I don't know whether it is the linen cupboard or the excitement or the whiskey.

JOAN Very well, Grant, but for the last time, mind you.

FORTESCUE In the Dyke[30] at eleven, as usual.

JOAN Yes, but now go or we'll be caught. Goodness, here's somebody.

[*Just as* FORTESCUE *reaches the dining-room door,* JACKSON *comes in by the other door.*]

JACKSON Joan, your father—Good gracious, who's this?

JOAN Oh, doctor, this is a friend of mine. Grant, you'd better go.

JACKSON Aren't you going to introduce me?

FORTESCUE I'm afraid I'm in a hurry. [*Opens the door.*]

---

30. *the Dyke* The Mardyke.

JACKSON Young man, come back. Come back, I say. May I introduce myself then? Jackson, Dr. Jackson.

JOAN His name's Lieutenant Fortescue. Now please let him go.

JACKSON I suppose Joan's father hasn't had the pleasure of your acquaintance?

FORTESCUE Joan, what right has Dr. Jackson—?

JOAN Grant! Please! I'll explain everything afterwards.

JACKSON Very well then. Good night, Lieutenant.

FORTESCUE Would you like me to stay and help you, Joan?

JOAN No, thanks. Now go!

[He does. There is a silence.]

JACKSON Well, young woman?

JOAN I suppose you'll tell father now?

JACKSON Why should I? I'm your godfather, amn't I? How long have you known this young man?

JOAN For a couple of months. We met accidentally.

JACKSON Oh, and I suppose I should ask what his intentions are?

JOAN He wants to marry me.

JACKSON Quite sure he's not married already?

JOAN Corney! You don't think he is?

JACKSON No, I'm merely pointing out that there are occasions when even fathers come in useful. And you?

JOAN What do you mean? Me?

JACKSON Are you in love with him?

JOAN Certainly not.

JACKSON Do you want to marry him?

JOAN Of course I don't. What would my father say? Corney, there's nothing like that. Honest, there isn't. We're friends, that's all.

JACKSON And what do you find attractive about this— friend of yours?

JOAN Well, he knows such a lot of things I don't know. He's travelled a good deal and he knows a great many interesting people.

JACKSON Yes.

JOAN *[eagerly]* But then he knows so little about other things.

JACKSON For instance?

JOAN   About Ireland, about us.

JACKSON   That's scarcely a definition of ignorance, Joan.

JOAN   But he doesn't understand how splendid we are. He thinks we're all so dull, and he doesn't see what a wonderful mind Mr. Hegarty has.

JACKSON   Ah, so you're attracted by Ned Hegarty too? Are you happy, Joan?

JOAN   Why, of course I am. What did you think?

JACKSON   Very happy?

JOAN   Naturally. . . . Corney, what are you suggesting? You're putting doubts into my mind. Aren't you happy, Corney?

JACKSON   What? I'm only joking, child. Putting doubts into your mind, indeed.

[O'LEARY comes in.]

O'LEARY   Joan, you're wanted to sing a song. Come on, hurry.

JOAN   I don't want to sing, Daddy. Get Mr. Hegarty to sing.

O'LEARY   He won't sing till you sing first. Sing one of them little French things the nuns taught you just to show 'em all what you can do.

JOAN   They're Italian, not French.

O'LEARY   Sure, aren't they all the same? Come on! Come on, Corney, You're like a fish out of water. You won't drink and you won't sing.

JACKSON   No, stay here a moment. I want to talk to you. Cut along, Joan.

JOAN   Corney, if you tell Daddy—

JACKSON   What do you take me for, Joan? Run along now.

[JOAN exits.]

JACKSON   Well, now, what's this about Hegarty?

O'LEARY   Ah, let me alone. I'm near out of me mind.

JACKSON   What is it?

O'LEARY   I was hoping to get it all settled tonight.

JACKSON   A match between him and Joan.

O'LEARY   Yes. I don't know what's wrong with the young men of today.

JACKSON   Do you mean that puppy refuses to marry her?

O'LEARY   Ah, more or less, more or less.

JACKSON   But this is outrageous.

O'LEARY   Ah, now there was nothing in writing. Before he went to gaol he asked me. And I agreed—more or less.

JACKSON   Did you even consult Joan?

O'LEARY   Of course I did but she'll do what I tell her.

JACKSON   I see. You might just as well not have consulted her at all.. And when you put it up to him the young rascal had changed his mind?

O'LEARY   Not even that, Corney. I wouldn't mind that so much, but he says 'tis on account of Coghlan's son. I can't make head nor tail of it. He says Jer Coghlan is in love with her too, and so on account of being so fond of Coghlan, he wouldn't break his heart, and Coghlan won't make any advances not to break his heart and—in all your born days, Corney Jackson, did you ever hear such a rigmarole? I don't know am I in my right mind.

JACKSON   It serves you right for cheapening your daughter to him.

O'LEARY   But isn't he a steady boy that would make a good husband for anyone? And aren't they all saying he have a great future before him when the country's free?

JACKSON   He has two lips that don't meet and two eyes that don't match, and I wouldn't be a bit surprised if your grandchildren turned out to be idiots.

[Pause.]

O'LEARY   Tell me, Corney, what would you think of Coghlan's boy? Old Dan must have pots of money, and they say young Jer has a great future before him at the bar. Maybe now he wouldn't be such a bad head to her.

JACKSON   Merciful God, after throwing the girl at the head of one man and having her rejected are you now suggesting doing the same thing with Coghlan?

O'LEARY   Sure I'm only making a suggestion. Can't you give me credit for what I'm trying to do?

JACKSON   You're no fit guardian for that child. You're a danger to her. She should have a woman to look after her. [Goes to the bell and rings.]

O'LEARY   What are you doing?

JACKSON   I want you to ask your sister to come and live with you.

O'LEARY Sure she detests the living sight of me. I asked her a dozen times to come and live with me and she wouldn't.
[NELLIE enters.]
JACKSON Nellie, if Miss O'Leary is below ask her whether she could come up here for a moment.
NELLIE Yes, sir. [Exit.]
O'LEARY Oh, she'll be there, she'll be there. That's the sort she is. And she'll walk out of the house, without bidding me the time of day.
JACKSON Will you allow me to speak to her?
O'LEARY I tell you she won't listen to you.
JACKSON We're old friends. I'll soon make her listen to me.
[KATE enters.]
JACKSON Kate, your brother has a favour to ask of you. He'll tell you himself what it is.
O'LEARY I've told the doctor already I asked you a dozen times and you refused.
KATE You mean give up the little shop and live here?
O'LEARY You can't be making so much out of the shop.
KATE 'Tisn't what I'm making, but what it gives me to do.
O'LEARY Well, will you do what I ask?
KATE No.
O'LEARY Why not?
KATE Because you and me never got on.
JACKSON For your mother's sake. She's old, and failing fast.
KATE Cady and me wouldn't get on, and Cady's daughter and me wouldn't get on. He may not have educated her out of her own knowledge[31] but he educated her out of mine. And furthermore, and what clinches it, is that I wouldn't get on with Cady's friends, the Hegartys and Coghlans and the other political blowholes.
O'LEARY Aren't you the bitter cantankerous old pill? Can't you let bygones be bygones? Woman alive, you can't go on living in the year 1867.
KATE Can you give me back my youth?
O'LEARY Only God can do that.

---

31. *educated her out of her own knowledge* So that she is no longer the same person.

KATE Even God can't give me back the man that was worth a hundred of your friends, and their leader, the picker-up of English prostitutes!

JACKSON Tush, tush, woman! Don't lose your temper.

O'LEARY For two pins I'd kick you down them stairs.

KATE You wouldn't have the courage.

O'LEARY What you wanted was a man to give you a damn good beating.

JACKSON This is outrageous. Kate, you should be ashamed of yourself. Cady, leave the room. I want to speak to your sister alone.

[O'LEARY *goes out scowling, cheerfully.*]

KATE Well, a fat lot of chance there is the pair of us could live together.

JACKSON For Joan's sake you must live together, for the sake of that young girl's future. You've allowed her to be brought up without a woman's care and if you don't like her you've only yourself to blame. Your brother will wreck her life if you're not careful. It's your duty to watch over her and see that she doesn't behave like a little fool.

KATE I couldn't do it, doctor, that's flat. I'm too old a dog to learn new tricks. I can only like them that like me; you know the sort of temper I have. I'm a hard woman to get on with.

JACKSON If you devote one tenth of the energy to winning her confidence that you've wasted on all the streels[32] of the city, that hang round your shop, you'll find her as affectionate as any daughter. Please, Kate.

KATE [*after a pause*] No.

[*From outside the noise of a crowd.*]

JACKSON [*angrily*] What the devil is all the uproar about. I declare I can't hear myself speak. [*Opens door.*] What is it? What are you all congregated there for? Cady, what is it? I can't hear you, man. Come in.

[O'LEARY *comes in; he is highly excited.*]

O'LEARY There's a split.

JACKSON A what?

O'LEARY The Party's split! They're after throwing over Parnell.

---

32. *streels* Slovenly women. From Irish *sraoill* = a slattern.

JACKSON Ah, I rather expected that.

[HEGARTY *comes in.*]

HEGARTY Our precious party—because of the divorce case. Coming to heel when Gladstone cracked the whip. Great God!

O'LEARY The country is split; split like Moses' Rock.

[COGHLAN *comes in.*]

COGHLAN It's London that does it; London drives them mad; the luxury, the wealth, the wire-pulling. What are they but farmers' sons, and small shop-keepers? Beggars on horseback riding to the devil!

HEGARTY It's incredible. It's monstrous. It's beyond belief, throwing over Parnell to satisfy the English.

COGHLAN Oh God, wait till we get them back! Wait till we get them back and we'll give them a warm welcome.

JACKSON Young man, young man!

COGHLAN The women of the lanes[33] will tear them asunder.

JACKSON Don't be too sure it isn't yourself they'll tear.

COGHLAN Do you think the common people will turn on Parnell, the man who made men of them, who beat down an Empire for them?

HEGARTY And just when freedom was in our grasp, just as we were beginning to plan for the future.

COGHLAN Jackson, do you think for an instant the people of Ireland will abandon Parnell?

JACKSON You know what I think of your democracies. Call out the lanes, but don't be too sure you can control them.

COGHLAN You'll see your mistake.

HEGARTY Yes, it won't stop us, it mustn't stop us. They'll have to go, every man of them.

JACKSON And remember there is always another power bidding for your democracy when it's on the warpath. Don't forget the Church.

COGHLAN To hell with it!

O'LEARY Oh, now, now, now!

COGHLAN Down with it, away with it, if it gets in our way. My own brother is a priest, and if he dared to interfere I'd say as much to him.

---

33. *the lanes* The poorest districts of Cork.

[Band begins to play "A Nation Once Again".[34]]
O'LEARY   Oh, Mother of God, more trouble.
COGHLAN   What is it?
O'LEARY   The band. 'Twas a little surprise I had in store for ye. Oh, couldn't they choose any other tune but that! Nellie! Nellie! Go and tell them fellows to stop.
HEGARTY   If the worst comes we can save our honour as they did in '67. It would be better than to see the cause of Ireland dragged in the mud of Westminster.
COGHLAN   Nonsense, Ned. Don't be so pessimistic. I tell you we'll show them who's master. You must organise a series of monster meetings. We must get in before them. We'll defeat them at the polls.
[NELLIE enters.]
NELLIE   Sir, sir, the band won't stop. They say they're engaged to play for half an hour.
JACKSON   Well, shut the window for God's sake, we can't hear ourselves speak.
[KATE closes window. BIDDY, SHUVAUN and SORRY come in. Everyone is at the window now looking down at the crowd below, except JACKSON, who remains aloof and cynical, and SHUVAUN.]
BIDDY   What is it, Mr. Hegarty, my love? There's crowds out. They're shouting and raving like lunatics.
COGHLAN   What did I say? What did I say? The whole country will be behind us.
SORRY   Ah, I was afraid of something like this. Whenever people gets too high in themselves, there's always trouble in store.
SHUVAUN   But the potatoes?
BIDDY   There's nothing wrong with the potatoes.
SHUVAUN   I thought it was the potatoes.
BIDDY   Poor creature, whatever'd go wrong, she'd think 'twas the blight.
SHUVAUN   The day in Ummera when the potatoes blackened a horseman went out and rode all day. Rode all day and never saw a green shoot.

---

34. *"A Nation Once Again"*.   A popular patriotic song written by Thomas Davis (1814–1845). It looks forward to the time when Ireland will be self-governing, and will no longer be "a province," but will once again be "a nation."

70

KATE Mother, mother, 'tisn't the potatoes. 'Tis the party. They're after turning against Parnell.

SHUVAUN What is it, Kate? I never saw you crying before. Is it anything bad they're after doing?

KATE Doctor, I was an old fool. I'll give up the shop, too long I kept it.

JACKSON Ah, now we're coming to the truth.

[JOAN comes in.]

JOAN What are you all doing in here? What's the meaning of the crowd?

COGHLAN It's nothing much, Joan, nothing very dreadful. A split in the Party.

JOAN Is that all? Goodness, I thought it was something serious!

CURTAIN

ACT TWO

[Scene: the same as before. It is an evening in the summer of 1891. KATE *is sewing.* JOAN *comes in; she wears a hat and gloves and carries some parcels.]*

KATE   Where were you, Joan?

JOAN   Doing the shopping for tomorrow.

KATE   I thought Nellie was to do that.

JOAN   Poor Nellie was so busy. I thought I'd give her a hand. Besides I wanted to call into the chapel.

KATE   Oh, you were up early this morning too.

JOAN   Yes, I wanted to get early Mass at the convent.

KATE   You don't always do that, do you?

JOAN   Not always.

KATE   Getting serious, maybe?

JOAN   I'm not a child any longer, Aunt Kate.

KATE   You weren't thinking of entering a convent by any chance?

JOAN   Well, to tell you the truth, I was.

KATE   I rather thought so.

JOAN   How did you know?

KATE   Well, if a girl of eighteen gets up at six in the

morning and sings hymns half the day, and does messages[35] no one asked her to do and makes everyone else as uncomfortable as possible, it's a safe assumption that she's thinking of entering a convent.

JOAN [meekly] I didn't know I was making anyone uncomfortable. I'm sorry. I'll try not to for the future.

KATE And 'tis also a safe assumption that a convent will never see her. [JOAN pauses as though to give a saucy answer, then bows her head again and goes.] Now what the devil is wrong with that girl?

[After a moment FORTESCUE is heard arguing with NELLIE. He bursts into the room, followed by NELLIE.]

FORTESCUE [off] But I tell you I saw her. She went in here. [Comes in.] I beg your pardon.

KATE And who are you, may I ask?

NELLIE I told you Miss Joan wasn't in.

FORTESCUE But I saw her, I followed her. She came in not two minutes ago. I must speak to her.

NELLIE My God! The master is downstairs. Will you speak low and get out? We'll be all kilt.

KATE What is it, I say?

NELLIE This gentleman is a follower of Miss Joan's.

FORTESCUE A friend of Miss Joan's. Fortescue, Lieutenant Fortescue. I'm sorry for disturbing you but I simply must see Joan. Are you her aunt?

KATE I am.

FORTESCUE Then do you mind my seeing her?

KATE I do.

FORTESCUE All I want is to know what she has against me.

KATE The same thing I have against you, maybe.

FORTESCUE Then tell me what is it, in heaven's name?

KATE Mr. Lieutenant whatever-your-name-is, I never thought I'd have the pleasure of telling your likes to get out of a house of mine, but I have it now and I'm not going to deny it to myself.

FORTESCUE Won't you tell me what I've done?

KATE The last time a uniform like yours stood under the same roof with me was twenty-five years ago and the man

---

35. messages Errands, especially odds and ends of shopping.

that went away from me never came back. Now, maybe you understand.

[JOAN *comes in. She has removed her outdoor clothes.*]

JOAN   Aunt Kate, what's all this about? Lieutenant Fortescue, how dare you come in here?

FORTESCUE   I've been waiting about this road all the evening for nothing else except to see you. Joan, I can't stand it any longer. I don't know why you're so cruel to me. You don't answer my letters.

JOAN   I wrote to you over a week ago and told you once for all I couldn't see you again. Isn't that enough?

FORTESCUE   But you gave me no reason.

JOAN   Oh, haven't we been over the reasons a hundred times, already? First, I don't want to marry you; second, even if I did my father wouldn't let me marry you; third, I'm going to marry someone else.

FORTESCUE   I don't believe you're such a fool.

KATE   You have a high opinion of yourself.

JOAN   Aunt Kate, don't interfere.

FORTESCUE   Joan, there's a dance at the barracks tonight. Come with me.

JOAN   No, no, no. I'm not going to any dances with you. I'm going to the Opera House tonight and even if I weren't I still wouldn't go with you. I wouldn't go within yards of your barracks. I don't know what you mean by forcing your way into this house, but I wish you'd find your way out again.

NELLIE   My God, if the master comes in, we'll all find our way out.

FORTESCUE   Well, I wish he would come in. I want to see him and find out if he's such a terrible monster as you're all hinting. I'll ask him straight if he has any objections to my marrying his daughter and see what they are. I'm sick of this. When I ask what's wrong with me, I'm told about what somebody or other did twenty-five years ago or in the days of Queen Anne.[36] I want to know what's wrong with *me*. Mind you, I know I'm not much good, but I want to be told my own faults, not somebody else's, and that's all anybody ever

---

36. *the days of Queen Anne.*   Perhaps an allusion to the expression "Queen Anne is dead," which was used as an ironic response to a piece of stale news.

tells me about. Just because somebody chopped off a priest's head a hundred years ago, I'm blamed for it. I tell you I never chopped off a priest's head, I don't want to chop off a priest's head, I don't want to chop off anybody's head. Does anyone think I do?

NELLIE *[in disgust]* I wouldn't put it apast you. *[Goes out slamming the door.]*

JOAN And now will you go? You see how you're upsetting everybody.

FORTESCUE I see I'm not going to be told what I've done.

JOAN You haven't done anything, but it's no use fighting against circumstances. Things are that way and you and I can't change them.

FORTESCUE Well, you're changing anyhow. That's not how you spoke to me before. You're sorry, aren't you, that things are that way? You'd like them to be different.

JOAN Perhaps I would.

FORTESCUE You're softening towards me, I can see that. Give me another month and I'll convince you that I'm right. Mind, Joan, the day will come when you'll regret this if you leave me now.

JOAN I can't help that. No matter how much I regret it, I'm not going to upset my father and my family for you. We'd better part now.

FORTESCUE You won't see me again.

JOAN No.

KATE And now you've had your answer, clear out.

FORTESCUE I haven't had my answer, and don't you believe I have. I'll go now, but Joan will think differently in a month or two.

KATE I'd rather Lee water had her[37] than one of your kind.

FORTESCUE When that's the only alternative you'll think differently too. *[Pauses a moment, and then goes out, slamming the door after him.]*

KATE Well, young woman?

JOAN Well?

---

37. *I'd rather Lee water had her* I'd rather she drowned in the River Lee. Cork is situated on the Lee.

KATE A Kerry convent—two heads on one pillow?

JOAN You needn't laugh; I mean it.

KATE You wouldn't want to marry that specimen?
[Pause.]

JOAN Jer Coghlan asked me to marry him.

KATE And what did you say to that?

JOAN Nothing. 'Tis hard to know what to say. I'm going to the opera with him tonight.

KATE Isn't he going to Parnell's meeting?

JOAN No, some way he doesn't seem to be so strong on Mr. Parnell as he used to be.

KATE And what about Ned Hegarty?

JOAN He doesn't seem to be such friends with Ned either. Ah, 'tis queer. Everything seems to be changing. I think I'll enter a convent after all.

KATE Somehow I don't think you will.

JOAN I think there must be great peace in a convent. I used to think the world was a grand place but now I'm not so sure. Everything turns out contrary. I used to think this was a grand city. Maybe Grant was right after all. Maybe 'tis nothing but a small mangy old place. Maybe—Aunt Kate, you don't like Jer Coghlan or Ned, do you?

KATE Not to put a tooth in it,[38] I do not.

JOAN Well, I do. I'm sure they're grand men. Everybody says they are.

[NELLIE comes in.]

NELLIE There's a man at the door, miss.

KATE What class of man is he?

NELLIE He's no class, miss, if you ask me. He have a game leg.

KATE 'Tis poor Dan Connors.

NELLIE Connors he said the name was, miss.

KATE Wisha, poor Dan, isn't it remarkable the way he found me out. *[KATE goes out.]*

NELLIE Well, she settled herself in all right. One'd think she owned the place.

JOAN She's very nice. I thought she'd be different. She used to be so bitter whenever I went into the shop.

NELLIE Ay, she's settling down nicely. If only she'd

---

38. *Not to put a tooth in it,* To speak openly.

keep them cronies of hers away. There were three of them in the kitchen last night . . . drinking the master's whiskey.

JOAN   If he finds out, there'll be a terrible row.

NELLIE   Ah, he met his match at last.

[O'LEARY *comes in.*]

O'LEARY   Nellie, who's that fellow I seen coming in here now?

NELLIE   A friend of Miss Kate's, sir. Dan Connors is the name.

O'LEARY   That fellow's a notorious bad character. I declare to my goodness I don't know what sort of people does Miss Kate associate with at all? Nellie!

NELLIE   Yes, sir.

O'LEARY   Any time you'd be answering the door you should turn the likes of him away. Do you hear?

NELLIE   *[stiffly]* Yes, sir.

O'LEARY   Tell them they're not wanted. There's no need to be announcing them at all.

NELLIE   I see.

O'LEARY   I don't want the house turned upside down on me. Now, go down and see what they're up to.

NELLIE   Very well, sir.

O'LEARY   And Nellie, who was drinking my whiskey? The bottle's empty.

NELLIE   I'm sure, I couldn't say, sir. I wasn't. *[Goes out.]*

O'LEARY   There's a saucy look for you. I suppose she has a fellow coming in. But I'll soon find that out.

JOAN   Are you going to the meeting?

O'LEARY   What meeting?

JOAN   Mr. Parnell's, of course. Isn't he coming here tonight?

O'LEARY   Of course I'm going. That's if I can throw off this bit of a cough. I wouldn't like to be out in the damp with that on me.

JOAN   Would you bring me?

O'LEARY   I would not indeed, bring you. What notion is this? Is that what I educated you for?

JOAN   I'd like to see Mr. Parnell.

O'LEARY   Now, you stop at home and keep your Aunt Kate company.

JOAN I'm not stopping at home. I'm going to the opera with Jer Coghlan.

O'LEARY With who, did you say?

JOAN With Jer Coghlan. Is there anything queer about that?

O'LEARY There's something very queer about it. I thought Coghlan was a red-hot Parnellite.

JOAN Well, he's not very hot now anyway.

O'LEARY My God, there's something I don't like about this. 'Tis your poor mother I should have instead of you— God rest her soul this night. "Burrow under the sea," she used to say, "and there'll be a Coghlan under you." There's only one meaning to that. He's clearing out for Father Henry's sake.

JOAN And why wouldn't he? Isn't one side as good as another?

O'LEARY Would you marry Jer Coghlan if he asked you?

JOAN He did ask me.

O'LEARY And what did you say?

JOAN I said nothing at all.

O'LEARY He'd make a fine match.

JOAN Will you never be done scheming?

O'LEARY Sure, someone have to scheme. His father must be worth a mint of money. I'd never need to put me hand in me pocket once the wedding was over.

JOAN I don't want to marry Jer Coghlan.

O'LEARY He'd be a better match for you than Ned Hegarty. The doctor was saying Hegarty wasn't well-balanced. He said his eyes didn't match. I don't know will I go to that meeting at all.

JOAN I'm not going to marry Ned Hegarty either for your information.

O'LEARY Well, may God pity me with you! Here am I nearly driven off my head trying to get a good husband for you and all you do is sniff. Why doesn't someone write a story about an unfortunate man trying to get his daughter settled? 'Tis Kate I blame for this. She have you addled with her romancing.

JOAN I never talked to Aunt Kate about it. I have too much respect for her.

O'LEARY Well, now, don't let her have any say in it.

Your Aunt Kate have great faults, Joan. I'm not satisfied with her. I don't know will she suit her position at all.
[Enter NELLIE.*]*
NELLIE   Miss Kate is just gone downstairs with a pair of your breeches, sir.
O'LEARY   My breeches? Which pair? Which pair?
NELLIE   The striped ones. A present for Dan Connors.
O'LEARY   Almighty Lord God, me second best breeches! Nellie, run after her quick. Tell her I want them back.
NELLIE   I told her that already, sir.
O'LEARY   Well, what did she say?
NELLIE   She said she'd give you a loan of a skirt if you ran short.
O'LEARY   A loan of a—you impudent thing! *[To* JOAN.*]* In my own house! *[To* NELLIE.*]* What are you laughing at? Me second best breeches!
JOAN   *[at the window]* That's Ned and the doctor. 'Twill be to fetch you to the meeting.
O'LEARY   I'm not going to any meeting. I feel too sick. Nellie, run down and tell them I'm gone.
NELLIE   Yes, sir. *[Exits.]*
JOAN   It's too late. Aunt Kate is after letting them in.
O'LEARY   Well, the divil fly away with her! I'm not even allowed to choose me own company.
[DR. JACKSON and HEGARTY come in, dressed for the meeting.]
HEGARTY   Such an evening, Mr. O'Leary.
O'LEARY   Night, Corney, Yes, 'tis very damp.
HEGARTY   Ah, I don't mean that. I mean the excitement. There's great news.
O'LEARY   I was just saying to Joan, I'm afraid I won't be able to go to the meeting. I have a bad throat.
HEGARTY   Oh, that's too bad. That's terrible. You mustn't miss it. Let the doctor look at your throat.
O'LEARY   I wouldn't bother him.
JACKSON   It's no bother. Let's see. *[Looks at* O'LEARY*'s throat.]* Yes, there's a little nervous inflammation. You should take a stiff glass of whiskey.
O'LEARY   And how the divil am I to take a stiff glass of whiskey with robbers under me own roof drinking me whiskey on me?

JACKSON I have a flask. Have you a warm scarf?

O'LEARY You don't think I ought to stop at home? Standing on a platform on a wet night would give a cold to the Father Mathew Statue.[39]

JACKSON Ach, there's no need. Ned and the boys are relying on you.

HEGARTY I'm so glad, Mr. O'Leary. It would be terrible to miss such an historic event. Did you hear? This morning before he caught the train Parnell burst in the offices of United Ireland. That's the way to deal with those traitors.

O'LEARY Oh, God, our poor country! 'Tis civil war.

JOAN I want to go to the meeting, but Daddy won't let me.

O'LEARY How can I, and you after promising to go to the opera with Jer Coghlan?

HEGARTY With Jer Coghlan?

O'LEARY Yes, there's a patriotic young hero for you.

HEGARTY Joan, are you sure about this? Isn't it possible you've made a mistake?

JOAN No, he asked me to go to "Princess Ida"[40] tonight, but I'd rather go to the meeting. Would you take me, Ned?

HEGARTY I can't believe Jer would leave us at a moment like this.

O'LEARY I was only saying, 'tis scandalous the way that fellow is trying to slink out of it; the miserable little hypocrite, letting on he couldn't reconcile it with his conscience when all knows 'tis the way old Dan Coghlan wouldn't like it fearing it might injure the business and Father Henry's promotion. Oh, I've been shockingly disappointed in that young man. God knows some people have no honour or decency.

JOAN Well, as no one wants to take me to the meeting, I'd better go and dress.

[JOAN goes out.]

JACKSON Do I hear the death knell of a great friendship?

HEGARTY Doctor, I still can't believe it. I know he hasn't been turning up to meetings, but I supposed it was the rush of business in the Land Courts. Do you believe it?

---

39. *the Father Mathew Statue.* A prominent Cork landmark. Father Mathew was a 19th century temperance leader.

40. *"Princess Ida"* A light opera written by the very popular team, librettist W. S. Gilbert (1836–1911) and composer Sir Arthur Sullivan (1842–1900).

JACKSON Let us ask himself.

HEGARTY If such a thing happened, I should lose my faith in human nature.

JACKSON You'll be lucky if that's all you lose.

HEGARTY What do you mean?

JACKSON You'll lose the girl and the election. Are you expecting a big crowd tonight?

HEGARTY An enormous crowd. I tell you, doctor, this is going to be an historic meeting. It will be the turn of the tide. Dublin this morning, Cork tonight, tomorrow it will be all Ireland.

O'LEARY Are you sure of that, Ned?

HEGARTY As sure as I am of my eternal salvation. The people are solid behind Parnell. They're only waiting for someone to show a lead.

O'LEARY I'm relieved to hear that, though I never had any doubts about it. None at all. Sure no one could be malicious enough to turn on a leader like Parnell just because of a bit of bother over a woman.

JACKSON That's not the way it is, judging by the reports we get from Carlow.

HEGARTY That means nothing. No one takes any notice of a by-election, and, besides, Carlow was never up to much.

JACKSON All the same, don't forget it may have an influence.

HEGARTY I know, I know. That's another reason we want a triumphal procession tonight. It may have an effect, even on Carlow.

JACKSON Maybe, maybe; for my part I back the Bishops' Manifesto every time.

HEGARTY The day is over when the priests can command the day in Irish politics. The people have grown up in the past ten years. The Land League has put spunk into them.

JACKSON Young man, young man, since the time I was that height, I'm hearing enthusiastic young men declare that the day of the priest in politics is over, and that the people have got some spunk in them at last. And those words, young man, have almost inevitably provided the epitaph for the young men that said them. Believe me, the priests always have the last word.

HEGARTY Don't you think the people are ever going to stand on their own? Don't you see any signs of progress?

O'LEARY In the name of goodness, Corney, why did you join the party with notions like that?

JACKSON That's exactly what I've been asking myself all this blessed evening. And the only reply I can think of is that there's no fool like the old fool.

HEGARTY Never mind the doctor, Mr. O'Leary. It's just that he enjoys being pessimistic. He's an old aristocrat and it gives him the shudders to rub shoulders with Paddy and Johnny. But his heart is sound all the same.

O'LEARY But no one likes knocking round with poor people the way he does. Sure, if only he'd mind his practice and stop working for nothing he could make a fortune.

JACKSON It's probably because I like Paddy and Johnny so much that I like to see them in their place.

O'LEARY My goodness, it's very serious if what you say is true. I don't know would we be right at all to stand up against the whole country.

[Enter KATE.]

KATE Cady, Nellie just told me you're after putting the whiskey under lock and key.

O'LEARY And who's better entitled? So 'tis you that was running away with my whiskey?

KATE I'm going to entertain my friends when they come to see me.

O'LEARY And who is it now?

KATE Peter Kenefick-O'Mahoney.

O'LEARY My God, that dirty little hobbler. Go away ou' that![41]

KATE Hand over those keys.

O'LEARY Corney, Corney, this was your idea, letting this one loose in my house.

JACKSON Here, Kate, there's half a flask left for Peter Kenefick-O'Mahoney and I hope God gives you more sense and me more money.

[The bell rings.]

---

41. *Go away ou' that!* Go away out of that, i.e., stop what you're doing. Here, it means "Stop talking like that, what you're saying can't be true!"

O'LEARY That's Coghlan's ring. Where is that girl? Nellie!

JACKSON Well, Kate, you're settling down?

KATE I'm missing the shop. The shop was great life.

JACKSON Admit it now, you're getting fond of that girl.

KATE I suppose I am.

[Another ring.]

O'LEARY God bless my soul, what's the matter with that girl? Nellie!

KATE I'll answer it. *[She goes.]*

O'LEARY I'm keeping two of them down there eating their heads off and they won't even open the door.

JACKSON The hour before battle. Are you feeling nervous, Ned?

HEGARTY Why should I? We know one another since we were boys.

[NELLIE comes in.]

NELLIE What is it?

O'LEARY What the blazes do you mean by not answering the door?

NELLIE I'm not answering the door to any Coghlan dead or living.

O'LEARY What's the meaning of this?

NELLIE You know well the meaning, after that old show[42] Father Henry telling us we'd be damned to all eternity if we voted for Parnell. A month's notice I'll give you if I see any more seceders[43] like that caffler[44] coming to the house. *[She goes.]*

O'LEARY The whole world is upside down, upside down. I'm finished, Corney, finished. Me last tune is played. I'll go up to me bed and stop there till ye have it settled.

[COGHLAN comes in, dressed for the opera.]

COGHLAN Evening, Mr. O'Leary. Your sister told me to come straight in.

O'LEARY You're welcome, my boy, you're welcome. I'm going down to get the whiskey out of the whiskey cupboard. Under lock and key I have to keep it now. Robbed be

---

42. *that old show* That poseur, show-off, ridiculous fellow.

43. *seceders* Turncoats, people who are not loyal.

44. *caffler* Literally, a street urchin, but also a general term of abuse.

God, robbed in my own house; skirts and trousers; every bloody thing. I'm going out of my mind. *[Exit.]*

JACKSON I'd better let you alone. Your father is well, I hope.

COGHLAN He's nearly all right again—the same old trouble.

JACKSON He has another twenty years in him. Don't worry.

COGHLAN I suppose I ought to explain, doctor.

JACKSON You mean about your new medical adviser?

COGHLAN It was in order not to embarrass you. Father didn't want to make any change; you know he has a great admiration for you. It would be different if you'd send in a bill like anyone else. But after the strong line you took at the meeting we felt it wouldn't be fair to trespass on your kindness. . . . Oh, hang it! I feel rotten, but what can I say? You've changed such a lot in the past couple of months. Now, you're an out-and-out Parnellite!

JACKSON Yes, we've all changed quite a lot, haven't we? *[Exits.]*

HEGARTY So it's a crime to be a Parnellite, Jer?

COGHLAN Well, there's my brother to be considered.

HEGARTY You're not coming to the meeting?

COGHLAN No, I'm scarcely dressed for the occasion.

HEGARTY You weren't at the last two committee meetings either. And now tonight when you're needed more than ever you're—taking Joan to the opera.

COGHLAN Yes.

HEGARTY Well, I suppose this is the end of what I was fool enough to think a great friendship.

COGHLAN Oh, for God's sake don't start doing Saint Sebastian[45] as if you were after being sentenced to another six months. I know what I'm doing, and it's what you'd be doing if you had any eye for the future.

HEGARTY If you mean that we should throw Parnell over because of the Bishops—

COGHLAN My dear Ned, I never expect you to alter a

---

45. *doing Saint Sebastian* Acting like a martyr. St. Sebastian was killed by being shot with many arrows. He is often pictured in such a way that his wounds are clearly visible, so that Coghlan suggests Hegarty is making a public display of his unhappiness.

tittle[46] for anybody or anything. If the angels came down from heaven to announce the Last Judgement you'd ask them to wait till you'd finished canvassing for Parnell. Can't you have some sense?

HEGARTY Sense? And what about loyalty? God knows, you preached enough about it.

COGHLAN Sense, man, sense. That's what's going to count in this. The country has turned against Parnell; I didn't expect it, I must admit, but now that it has we must face the facts and try to get all we can out of the burning house. The most important thing at the moment is to hold on to the alliance with the Liberals.

HEGARTY So that was the goal of the national movement, to tie this country to the apron strings of an English political party?

COGHLAN When that Party is able and willing to give us Home Rule, yes. I'd take Home Rule from the hands of a Zulu Chief.

HEGARTY Much chance you have of getting Home Rule or anything else when you've destroyed the one man the English stand in dread of.

COGHLAN He destroyed himself when he sacrificed Ireland to an English prostitute.

HEGARTY And you say that, you who declared over and over that every man was entitled to his own private life.

COGHLAN As long as it remains his private life.

HEGARTY It is the end. I see now what a fool I was. And I suppose it's the same with Joan. That also was foolishness.

COGHLAN All's fair in love and war.

HEGARTY The new philosophy!

COGHLAN The realist philosophy. You know, Ned, we were both rather hysterical in the old days. I was as big a fool as you were, remember. Now, I'm out for what I can get in life and politics, I give you fair warning. I've asked Joan to marry me. Can't we be friends on the new terms? I'll call you all the names I can think of and we'll both meet and be good friends afterwards.

HEGARTY I don't want your friendship on the new

---

46. *a tittle* The least little bit.

terms. I shouldn't believe in it as I believed in the old. You've released me from my obligations.

COGHLAN And you won't shake hands?

HEGARTY No.

[JOAN *comes in, dressed for the opera.*]

JOAN I'm ready, Jer.

HEGARTY Joan, you said you wanted to come to the meeting tonight.

JOAN Yes. Why?

HEGARTY Will you come with me?

COGHLAN Joan is coming to the opera with me.

HEGARTY Let her answer for herself.

JOAN But I'm dressed for the opera, Ned.

HEGARTY It won't take you five minutes to change.

JOAN Have you two been having a row?

HEGARTY Joan, I put off asking you to marry me because of Coghlan's feelings. Now I don't give a damn for his feelings. Will you marry me now, Joan?

JOAN And what about my feelings? Or had you forgotten them?

HEGARTY Joan, I explained at the time. You know I didn't want to hurt you.

JOAN Oh, yes, you explained all right. I didn't understand then, but I do now. You sacrificed me to your passion for showing off. You see, you may have learned a lot in the last couple of months, but I've learned something too. I've learned that all those high-sounding sentiments of yours were so much posing. They took me in then as they took in yourself and everyone else, but they don't take me in now. And perhaps you'd understand this. I wouldn't marry either of you, not if there was no one else but the pair of you, not if I had to live all my life as an old maid in this stinking city, with humbugs and fools. Now, clear out, the pair of you, and let me alone. [*She goes to the window.*]

[HEGARTY *goes out, slamming the door behind him.*]

COGHLAN Joan, you and I are going to the opera.

JOAN Haven't I told you what I think of you? I'm not going to marry you, and I'm not going to the opera with you. Isn't that clear?

COGHLAN That's where you're wrong. You're going to do both.

JOAN You're being very impudent.

COGHLAN No, Joan, realistic. You don't want me to tell your father about your goings-on, do you?

JOAN What do you mean?

COGHLAN About this English officer you've been entertaining unknown to him.

JOAN How did you know?

COGHLAN Never mind. You were meeting him every day in the Dyke while Ned Hegarty was in gaol, weren't you? Ah, Joan, you're not such a little saint as you look, you know. Now, do you want me to tell your father who he is?

JOAN What do you know about him?

COGHLAN His name is Fortescue.

JOAN I know that.

COGHLAN And it doesn't mean anything to you?

JOAN No.

COGHLAN Well, I'm sorry if I have to break the news, but he is one of the greatest young blackguards in English society. Perhaps you don't remember the Maddington divorce case. The un-named correspondent[47] of Mrs. Maddington was a young man whose name was suppressed for very good reasons—his family were influential enough to have it suppressed. That young man was sent to Ireland to get him out of the way, and that precious young blackguard is the man you've been entertaining under your father's roof. Now, do you want me to tell him?

JOAN No, Jer, you mustn't. He'd murder me.

COGHLAN That would be the least thing that'd happen. If once a thing like that got out about you, your reputation would be gone forever.

JOAN I know, people are so cruel.

COGHLAN I see nothing cruel about it.

JOAN Of course, it's cruel. Think how that poor boy's life has been blighted by a little thing like that.

COGHLAN What sort of morality did they teach you at school?

JOAN Oh, don't be silly, Jer. It might have happened to anybody.

---

47. *correspondent* This is the spelling used in the MS. Joan's confusion in the following scene results from the similarity between *correspondent* and *co-respondent*, a person accused of adulterous relations with a spouse in a divorce suit.

COGHLAN I wonder have you any notion at all what I'm talking about.

JOAN Well, you said all he did was correspond with the other man's wife. . . . *[Pause.]* Or was it . . . ? *[Louder.]* Jer, was it like Mr. Parnell?

COGHLAN Exactly.

JOAN My God!

COGHLAN So now, Joan, I think for your own sake and your father's you will marry me.

JOAN Up to this I had some queer sort of hope. . . . I don't know . . . maybe after all I thought I might. . . . Now, everything seems to be knocked away from under me. Yes, I will marry you.

COGHLAN I think that's very sensible of you. I do indeed. You won't regret it.

[JACKSON and O'LEARY *come in.* O'LEARY *is wearing his overcoat.]*

JACKSON Now we're all set. Where's Hegarty?

COGHLAN He couldn't wait.

JACKSON That young man is too enthusiastic.

COGHLAN Mr. O'Leary. Joan and I are going to be married.

O'LEARY What's that?

COGHLAN It's true.

JACKSON Coghlan, for the first time in my life, I feel a little bit jealous.

O'LEARY That's the first bit of good news I had for months. Corney, we won't go to the meeting after all. Hegarty's away now and we can sit here and celebrate.

JACKSON No, no, let them alone. Joan, you haven't said a word yet. Aren't you pleased?

JOAN Very pleased, Corney.

JACKSON Be happy, enjoy yourself. Don't think of us old people. Think of the world before you and enjoy it while you can. There, there, you little fool, I didn't mean to make you cry.

O'LEARY Joan, child, I'm delighted. Didn't I always say you wouldn't disgrace me? I only wish your poor mother was here to share the good news. Mind her, Jer. She's a good girl.

COGHLAN I'll mind her, sir. Don't worry.

O'LEARY *[softly to* COGHLAN*]* I wouldn't be going to

this meeting, only I promised before the Bishops' Manifesto came out. D'ye see? 'Tis the last one. Tell your brother, Father Henry, that, the next chance you get.

COGHLAN I quite understand, Mr. O'Leary. We were all a bit tied up in our old loyalties.

O'LEARY Oh, Jer, my boy, little you know how happy you made me this night. I'll quench that lamp. There's no good in wasting it.

COGHLAN Will you wait until I call a cab, Joan?

JOAN I'll wait here.

COGHLAN I shan't be a minute.

JACKSON Good night, Joan.

JOAN Good night, Corney.

O'LEARY Good night, Joan, You don't want a light.

JOAN No, Daddy, I prefer the darkness.

[They go out. JOAN is by the window. The lighted tarbarrels[48] *send a weird light into the room. In the distance a band is heard. KATE and SHUVAUN enter.]*

KATE Look at that mangy caubogue[49] after quenching the lamp for fear we'd waste a ha'porth[50] of oil on him.

SHUVAUN Ah, the poor boy, he have great expinses.

KATE I'll give him more expenses. They're after lighting the tarbarrels. Will you look at the sky?

SHUVAUN Whisha, tell me, Chait, *inghean o,*[51] who are they cheering?

KATE They're cheering Parnell.

SHUVAUN And who is he? No one ever tells old Shuvaun anything. I suppose because she's getting feeble. Tell me, Chait, is it for the people he is?

KATE Ach, you wouldn't understand. 'Tis all different now.

SHUVAUN Cease your weeping now,
Women of the soft wet eyes.

---

48. *The lighted tarbarrels* Barrels of tar were burned to give light to public gatherings held outdoors after dark, especially when it was desired to create an atmosphere of celebration.

49. *caubogue* Ignorant fellow. From Irish *caobach*, which has the same meaning.

50. *ha'porth* Half-penny's worth.

51. *Chait, inghean o,* Irish = Kate, my daughter.

89

> Till Art O'Leary drink
> Ere he go to the dark house—[52]

KATE What's that?

SHUVAUN A lamint. A lamint for wan that was killed by the English in Carriganimma long ago. He was one of your father's people. . . . Did I hear the sound of crying, Chait?

KATE Almighty God have pity on that poor man! Have pity on our poor distracted people! Have pity on me that wasted my life in bitterness and don't let the lives of the young be wasted like mine.

[JOAN sweeps suddenly out of the room. The band is louder now, and lights flicker on the walls of the room.]

SHUVAUN I thought I heard someone go out.

KATE *[loudly and fiercely]* Almighty God, have pity on our poor people!

CURTAIN

---

52. *"Cease your weeping now . . ."* From an 18th century poem, "The Lament for Art O'Leary" written by Art O'Leary's wife Eileen. It is one of the most famous of the later poems written in the Irish language. Frank O'Connor produced a fine English translation of it.

ACT THREE

[Scene: the same. An evening October 1891, the day following Parnell's funeral.[53] *JOAN is standing by the window. KATE comes in; she carries some raisins and a duster.]*

KATE *[off]* Nellie! *[Comes in.]* Ah, Joan, couldn't you go upstairs and finish packing your trunks? Dan Connors is coming to bring it down to the station and you haven't done a hand's turn all night.

JOAN What's the hurry?

KATE What's the hurry? Are you getting married in the morning or am I? Or are you after forgetting about it?

JOAN Sure, isn't there a whole houseful to do that?

KATE A nice useful houseful they are. Now, Joan, like a good child run upstairs and finish the trunks. Nellie!

JOAN There's time enough.

KATE Oh, for pity's sake and pity's sake go and do something and don't stand mooning there on me.

[NELLIE comes in.]

NELLIE What is it, ma'am?

---

53. *An evening . . . funeral.* This wording is found in the MS. The program for the Abbey production has "ACT III - 12th October 1891."

KATE   How many times did I call you?

NELLIE   Now, Miss Kate, look here, instead of calling me 'twould be fitter for you to call all the others out of my way. There's Biddy Lally and Sorry Sullivan eating one another's heads off about politics and Cook can't get near the range to look at the cakes.

KATE   Mother of God, are they after turning politicians now? Take these raisins down to Cook and tell her it's a pound of sugar and a wine glass of port. And then come back and start laying the table.

NELLIE   Very well, Miss.

KATE   And when the master comes back send him into town again for another dozen of champagne. At least 'twill take him out of our way for a while.

[NELLIE goes out.]

Oh dear, oh dear, I wish I had you off my hands.

[BIDDY drags SORRY into the room; both are wearing aprons and caps.]

BIDDY   Lies, lies, lies, lies!

KATE   What's wrong with you?

BIDDY   What's wrong with her? Repeat your words, you blackvisaged old *bodach*.[54]

JOAN   I'll go up and finish my box. *[Exit.]*

BIDDY   Repeat your words, I say.

SORRY   Kate, she insulted me. She said I was in it only for what me son could get out of it.

BIDDY   And isn't it true for me? Didn't they give out the tickets for the porter in his name? Isn't that why you're such a great supporter of Father Henry's?

SORRY   I always liked Father Henry. A lovely man with a devotional countenance. Isn't he a better man to look to than a dirty Protestant whoremaster?

BIDDY   There! There! By God, I'll make you swallow that.

KATE   You should be ashamed of yourself, Sorry Sullivan, and have some respect for the dead.

SORRY   I'm true to my church, Kate Leary, true to my faith like I always was. When this world passes what else have we? Ah, Biddy Donoghue, I'll see you on the last day with

---

54. *bodach.*   Irish = ignorant old peasant.

the flames licking you for all the things you said against the cloth tonight.

KATE Come on, clear out, the pair of ye! I've no time to waste on you.

BIDDY The Chief's not dead! He'll come back, he'll come back and make ye eat yeer words.

SORRY Dead and damned and the cold hob of hell to his backside.

BIDDY 'Twasn't him they buried at all. 'Twas only a pretence because the English were out to kill him.

SORRY Mad, mad, that's what all of ye are! Mad in yeer hatred of God and His Church.

KATE Whisht, Biddy, whisht. He's dead, sure enough. The doctor and Mr. Hegarty are gone to Dublin for the funeral.

BIDDY I'll never believe it.

[KATE pushes them into the dining-room as O'LEARY comes in by the other door, followed by NELLIE.]

KATE And now be quiet the pair of ye, and give Nellie a hand with the table. Don't ye see the poor girl is demented?

O'LEARY What's this about? I come home played out and that strap of a girl orders me out for champagne.

KATE Well, it won't do you any harm to do a bit of work for once in a while.

NELLIE Dan Connors is below now, Miss.

[KATE goes out.]

O'LEARY What's that fellow after now?

NELLIE He came for Miss Joan's trunk to bring it to the station.

O'LEARY Ha! Seeing what he can pick up! Have he me trousers on him?

NELLIE He have.

O'LEARY That they may blister his backside.

[JOAN comes in.]

JOAN Where's Aunt Kate?

NELLIE Gone downstairs to Dan Connors. Did you finish your boxes?

JOAN I did.

NELLIE Do you know what I heard?

JOAN No.

NELLIE The regiment is off tonight—for India.

O'LEARY   What regiment is that?

NELLIE   Miss Joan knows. *[Exit.]*

O'LEARY   Since your Aunt Kate came to this house I'm getting nothing but impudence from the servants. Joan, if you hear anything unusual about me in the next few weeks, you'll understand 'tis for your sake.

JOAN   What are you driving at?

O'LEARY   There'd be something unnatural in you being married to a prominent Anti and me being the other way round.

JOAN   What difference will it make to me?

O'LEARY   Now, 'twill make a lot of difference. And besides I'm beginning to think the Coghlans backed the right horse after all. They're doing well out of it. I think I'd be well advised. Besides, there's the band. Peter Hurley the bandmaster is worried to death. He says they don't mind what side they take so long as they take some side.

JOAN   The doctor ought to be back for the wedding. Do you think he will?

O'LEARY   I don't know. I was thinking if I joined and brought the band with me 'twould be a powerful move. Father Henry have a great eye on the band.

JOAN   I'd like to have the doctor here.

O'LEARY   What the devil took him up to Dublin for the funeral? He must be getting soft.

JOAN   Himself and Ned Hegarty went up together.

O'LEARY   Running after lost causes!

JOAN   I wish he took me with him.

O'LEARY   Now, don't you go talking like that to the Coghlans. They'll have you well watched. Keep your mind to yourself like the Banveen.[55] And remember. Never contradict your husband. If he says black is white you say 'tis white. If he says the earth is flat say 'tis flat. I'm speaking to you now as if I was your mother.

[In the distance a band is heard approaching, playing a military march, "The British Grenadiers".]

---

55. *Keep your mind to yourself like the Banveen.*   A variant of an old saying, "Keep your mind to yourself like the bonav." Bonav = Irish *banbh*, pig; Banveen or bonaveen = Irish *banbhín*, piglet. It is not entirely clear why the pig should be thought a particularly secretive animal.

O'LEARY   Surely to God that's not my band. I told them not to stir out until morning when they play you to the station.
[NELLIE comes in.]
NELLIE   'Tis the soldiers. You can see them from this.
O'LEARY   And who gave you permission to come in here?
NELLIE   Ah, botheration to you, can't we even look out of the window?
[KATE comes in, and goes to JOAN and NELLIE at the window.]
KATE   What is it?
NELLIE   'Tis the regiment.
O'LEARY   I don't know what divil's interest women have in soldiers. One'd think a red coat was a pair of wings.
NELLIE   All the way to India they're going, imagine. Oh God, I wouldn't like to go all that distance from home.
KATE   Do you see anyone you know?
NELLIE   No, no. I thought for a minute that was him. Where is he at all?
O'LEARY   Who are ye talking about?
KATE   The big drummer. He's a friend of Nellie's.
O'LEARY   Don't let me see any English soldiers about this house. They're no good.
NELLIE   It's hard to see in the darkness. Don't the uniforms look lovely?
[A pause, then JOAN goes sadly away from the window.]
JOAN   They're gone.
O'LEARY   There'll be another one tomorrow.
NELLIE   Isn't it a lonely feeling seeing them go, all that long way?
KATE   Whisht, now, whisht, and go back to your work.
[NELLIE goes out into the dining-room.]
Joan, child, you're tired.
JOAN   Yes, I'm tired. I wish it was all over.
O'LEARY   'Twon't be long now.
[The door opens and HEGARTY enters. He is dishevelled and there is blood on his necktie.]
KATE   What is it?
HEGARTY   The doctor?
JOAN   What is it, quick?
HEGARTY   He's hurt.

JOAN Where is he?

HEGARTY There are two men bringing him along. I came on to prepare you.

JOAN Ned, is it serious?

HEGARTY I don't think so. They cut him up with their sticks.

JOAN Who did it?

HEGARTY Father Henry's boys—Chris Daly and his gang.

O'LEARY My God, the ones he nursed and physicked. I'll go down and help them up with him. *[Exit.]*

KATE And I'd better get out a couple of bandages.

JOAN Were you hurt, Ned?

HEGARTY No, only a scratch.

JOAN Chris Daly's gang—aren't they Jer's bodyguard?

HEGARTY I believe so. Why?

JOAN Nothing.

HEGARTY We both wanted to be down in time for the wedding; to wish you luck.

JOAN Thanks, Ned.

HEGARTY You know how I feel about you, how I'll always feel.

JOAN Will you always be the same, Ned?

HEGARTY Always. You will always be the one great thing in my life. In fifty years time if I live I shall see you standing before me as you stand now, and I shall think of the one great chance I missed.

JOAN Ned, you missed nothing. I'd have been a bad wife to you.

HEGARTY You know that's not true.

JOAN No, no, it is. I used to think at one time I'd have been a good one, I saw myself inspiring you to write poems, making you happy. But now—Ned, can you tell me what's happened to me within this last year? Have I changed beyond recognition?

HEGARTY No, of course you haven't. You'll never change.

JOAN But I have changed, Ned. That's what you don't understand. That's why I couldn't be a good wife to you any more. I'm changing under your very eyes. I changed a moment ago when you came in with that terrible story. I felt the chill at the pit of my stomach.

HEGARTY I shouldn't have told you.

JOAN It wouldn't have made any difference. It would happen in spite of you. People don't mean the same thing any longer, either that or they mean so much more. I used to think this house was so lovely, the river and trees. The whole city seemed beautiful like a garden. Now it seems a shabby, neglected place, a hideous place; mean, ugly, sordid. I'm sorry, Ned. You see I wouldn't be much use to you after all. I'd better go now and see if I can help Aunt Kate. *[Exit.]*

[O'LEARY and JACKSON come in.]

O'LEARY That's grand; you're doing fine. Now settle yourself till I get you a drop of whiskey.

HEGARTY How are you feeling, doctor?

JACKSON I'd feel better if I'd floored Chris Daly.

O'LEARY And to think of them turning on you, and the way you sat up night after night with their sick brats. 'Tis terrible, terrible. They'd turn on anyone now.

[KATE comes in.]

KATE Hallo, me poor warrior. You got hurt.

JACKSON I did.

KATE The blessings of God on you. I always said you lived too sheltered a life. Did you make them run?

JACKSON No, I did the running.

KATE Wisha, bad cess[56] to you! Give us a look at that head of yours. Nellie is bringing the water. I thought you were supposed to be in Dublin.

JACKSON They were waiting for me outside the station.

KATE I'll get you an old gun before you go. They'll be waiting for you.

JACKSON Somehow I don't think they will, though I got a bit of a fright at the front door. There was a suspicious looking customer hanging round.

KATE Is he there still?

JACKSON He slunk away when he saw us.

O'LEARY If that's one of Chris Daly's gang, I won't be long warning him off. Come down with me, Ned.

---

56. *bad cess* Bad luck.

HEGARTY Yes, I must be going anyhow. Goodnight, doctor. Goodnight, Miss O'Leary.

JACKSON Mind yourself.

HEGARTY I'll be safe.

[HEGARTY and O'LEARY go.]

KATE That fellow—what was he like?

JACKSON Tall and dark, well-dressed; do you know him?

KATE I think I can guess.

JACKSON Do you mean her soldier friend? But that's impossible. The regiment have left. They passed us on our way from the station.

KATE Perhaps he came back. Soldiers are very sentimental.

JACKSON Ah, the poor devil, the poor devil. Kate, run down like a decent woman and give him a couple of whiskies.

[NELLIE enters from the dining-room and goes out by the other door.]

NELLIE That fellow Coghlan is at the door! Suppose I shall have to let him in. *[Exit.]*

JACKSON I'd better go upstairs and wash some of this blood off. Besides I don't like that young man after tonight.

KATE Neither do I. I'll go and console that young lover. I gave him a bit of me tongue the last time we met.

JACKSON We'll go out this way; I don't want to meet him.

[KATE and JACKSON go out. After a moment COGHLAN and O'LEARY come in.]

COGHLAN I only just heard what happened at the station. It's terrible.

O'LEARY Well, it's no use talking to me about it. Talk to Dr. Jackson.

COGHLAN Well, he being such a friend of yours, I wanted to explain.

O'LEARY Was it you put them up to it?

COGHLAN Mr. O'Leary—you don't think that?

O'LEARY They were your followers, Father Henry's gang.

COGHLAN Father Henry is most upset. It was another man altogether they were after.

O'LEARY Ned Hegarty, I suppose.

COGHLAN   Well, as a matter of fact I believe it was. They seem to have a bit of a grudge against Hegarty. You understand, I had nothing to do with it. But still, 'tis most regrettable.

O'LEARY   And he supposed to be such a friend of yours. Well, well.

COGHLAN   Mr. O'Leary, don't let a mistake of that kind come between us. I promise you it won't ever occur again. I want to make an offer to you, Mr. O'Leary.

O'LEARY   What is it?

COGHLAN   You know we're anxious to have you on our side.

O'LEARY   Ye're not the only one.

COGHLAN   No, but we're the ones who're going to win.

O'LEARY   Sit down and take a drink.

COGHLAN   Thanks, I will. *[Takes a drink.]* Well, it's like this. We're in a grave difficulty about a candidate for the election and we were wondering whether you'd be prepared to help us. The sort of candidate we need is a man with influence and a good business to his back. A man who's popular. There'd be no doubt whatever about his success. The clergy will support him to a man, and his only opponents would be the old Fenians and a sprinkling of wild young men. The people won't dare to oppose the Church.

O'LEARY   Well?

COGHLAN   The only one the Parnellites have is Ned Hegarty.

O'LEARY   You came to make me an offer, you said.

COGHLAN   Would you stand against Hegarty?

O'LEARY   Me?

COGHLAN   Of course, we realise it would be more than a little awkward for you, but there are certain advantages as I think you'll recognise.

O'LEARY   Stand against Ned Hegarty. That's a serious matter, young man. I don't know could I do it, even if I wanted to. Ned is an old friend of mine.

COGHLAN   For the sake of Ireland, Mr. O'Leary.

O'LEARY   Oh, yes, of course, Ireland comes first. All my life I've sacrificed everything to the cause of Ireland. Still—if 'twas anyone else except Ned Hegarty. People might say things.

COGHLAN Remember Ireland, Mr. O'Leary.

O'LEARY Yes, yes, we must never forget old Ireland. I'll tell you what I'll do. I'll talk to Peter Hurley the band-master. Anything I do will have to be done in consultation with the band.

COGHLAN The band would be a very welcome acquisition.

O'LEARY Well now, keep it to yourself. Not a word about it till the wedding is over.

COGHLAN Not a word.

O'LEARY I'll send Joan in to you. I suppose you'll be wanting to see her.

COGHLAN I'd like to explain about the attack on Dr. Jackson.

O'LEARY Not a word to her though. She doesn't understand diplomacy.

COGHLAN You can trust my discretion.

[O'LEARY *goes out. A moment later* JOAN *enters.*]

Joan, I just came round to apologise to your father.

JOAN Did you set them on?

COGHLAN Of course not. How can you suggest such a thing?

JOAN Then why are you apologising?

COGHLAN Because those hooligans have attached themselves to our party.

JOAN Have you apologised to Ned?

COGHLAN I don't intend to. He'd only get what he deserves. He hasn't been any too gentle in the things he says about me.

JOAN And does that give you the right to set paid bullies on him?

COGHLAN By what right do you adopt this tone to me? How dare you suggest that I'm responsible!

JOAN Of course, you're responsible! Who put the sticks into the hands of the hooligans if it wasn't you? Who goes around saying your opponents are damned, but you?

COGHLAN I didn't ask for the split.

JOAN Of course you asked for it. You and Ned and all the others. All the pretence is broken down at last, and you can indulge all the meanness of your mean little souls, spitting in your neighbour's face, stealing his trade, plotting and intriguing against him, and all in the name of Ireland and religion.

COGHLAN Joan, you're forgetting yourself.

JOAN No, I'm only coming to myself. It's you who've made me so that I don't know any longer what happiness is; it's you who have made everything ugly for me. You, with your quarreling and spite and hate. It's just as well this happened, Jer. I don't want you to buy a pig in a poke.[57] I'm no longer the sort of convent school miss I used to be.

COGHLAN And the change is no improvement.

JOAN Well, that's another thing you'd better learn. I'm developing a thoroughly nasty temper and for the future you're going to feel the weight of it unless you improve your manners.

COGHLAN Joan, you're insufferable. There's no speaking to you. I hope by the time you reach the church you'll be ready to apologise.

[COGHLAN goes out, and KATE comes in.]

KATE That was a fine row you were having with your future husband.

JOAN I'll send Nellie up with a note. He wants me to apologise.

KATE I'd see him in hell first.

JOAN But, Aunt Kate, I can't go to the altar like this, as I am, after flying into such a rage. What sort of beginning would that be?

KATE Are you going to the altar with him, by the way?

JOAN Aunt Kate, what are you suggesting? You're not thinking, you're not really thinking I'd throw him over now? [Pause.] Aunt Kate, say something, can't you? [Pause. Peevishly.] You're such a queer woman, I never know what's in your mind. [Pause.] You hate him, don't you? You really detest him?

KATE There's someone waiting for you in your grandmother's room. Are you going to see him?

JOAN Aunt Kate, who is it?

KATE Who do you think?

---

57. *to buy a pig in a poke.* To enter on a course of action in ignorance. A "poke" is a bag.

JOAN It can't be him. We saw them marching past. Don't keep me in suspense. Is it?

KATE Yes. Will you go up to him?

JOAN No, no, no. I won't, I won't.

KATE Won't what?

JOAN I won't go away with him. He's a notorious bad character. He did terrible things.

KATE Then why did you keep going with him?

JOAN I couldn't get rid of him. I wrote to him twenty times breaking it off.

KATE Once is breaking it off. Twenty times is dragging it on.

JOAN I don't care. I won't do it. It would break Daddy's heart. It might ruin Jer's career. Once and for all I won't go away with him.

KATE Now, who asked you to go away with him?

JOAN What did you ask me then?

KATE Goodness gracious, is the child deaf? I asked you to go up and say goodbye to him. You kept him trailing after you long enough.

JOAN I won't, I won't.

KATE It's so queer you should think I wanted you to run away with him. I wonder now what put that into your head? Such a crazy notion. Run away with him the night before you were married? What would your father say?

JOAN Aunt Kate, what would he say?

KATE Oh, he'd say a lot, but that wouldn't worry me. But if you think 'twould break his heart—well, somehow I don't think it would. I don't really know what your father's heart is made of, girl, but I wouldn't say 'twas breakable stuff. And I wouldn't rely on breaking Mr. Jer Coghlan's either— or the irritation in his chest he calls a heart. Now if 'twas the doctor's, there's a heart you could break, if once he let you find it.

JOAN I couldn't, I couldn't.

KATE Well, if you couldn't, you couldn't, and that's all about it. I'll go and tell the poor boy not to wait.

JOAN Yes, do. No, don't. I'll tell him myself. Aunt Kate, I think you're fond of me.

KATE Sometimes I think the same myself.

JOAN You wouldn't advise me to do anything wrong.

You know so much of the world and I know so little. If I go to him now I may never come back. Do you think I'd be doing wrong? Very wrong?

KATE If you were itself, I wouldn't blame you. He's a decent boy. You'll come to no harm.

JOAN God direct me, I was never so tempted. I can't face it, life in this mean little town with this—

KATE Yes? What were you going to say?

JOAN I can't bring myself to say it.

KATE I'll say it for you: "this mean little man."

JOAN [comes and kneels beside KATE] Aunt Kate, I don't want to go but something seems to be driving me; I'm caught up in it. I can't stop myself. Aunt Kate, in case I don't come back—

[KATE kisses her. JOAN rises and goes out. Enter JACKSON.]

KATE Well, how's the warrior?

JACKSON Nicely, thanks. And the old Fenian?

KATE As big a Fenian as ever.

JACKSON I'm glad to hear it. I never thought much of the Fenians myself, but they were better men than their sons.

KATE I never thought much of doctors myself but they're better men than politicians. And by the same token, isn't it about time you stopped your kimeens?[58]

JACKSON My kimeens?

KATE Your gladhiatoring.[59]

JACKSON Oh, that's all over.

KATE 'Twas about time.

JACKSON Just about. When they sank the coffin in the grave a strange light came in the sky. I took it as a sign to put a stop to my gladhiatoring as you call it, and return to the peace of a middleaged and not very inspiring existence.

KATE And were you glad?

JACKSON Now that's the remarkable thing. I was thoroughly miserable. These Indian summers of middleaged men. Maybe you experienced something of the kind yourself?

KATE Maybe I did.

58. kimeens? Sly tricks. From Irish faoi choim = under cover, in secret.

59. gladhiatoring. Gladiatoring, i.e. fighting publicly, in this case for the Parnellite cause.

JACKSON Well, I hope it's all over and that you and I can enjoy our Sunday evening chat and our glass of grog.

KATE If it's not over, it soon will be.

JACKSON Yes, tomorrow we lose Joan. I shall miss her.

KATE But, you didn't tell me yet what started you off.

JACKSON What started me? How do I know? What does start people off on a jigmareel[60] like that? I know it began that night, you were here, weren't you—when word came of the split. I saw there was going to be an unholy stink and because there was no hope, because it was already doomed, that beautiful world of our imagination—what nonsense I'm talking.

KATE No, go on.

JACKSON *[rises and walks to the window]* Because the sun was setting and I'd never walked in the sun, and I knew when once 'twould set, 'twould set forever, for me.

KATE It set long ago for me.

JACKSON Yes.

KATE And when I saw it setting for others I was so sorry for them. There wasn't a stitch of the old bitterness left in me. I was as weak as a child. I went home and cried myself sick. It was like being born again. I saw everything different. I was so sorry, even for Cady, that I came back to him.

JACKSON Maybe you can tell me why it happens us?

KATE Ach, sure what are we but poor people? What do we know of the world? Sure we only came into it in my lifetime. We're only learning to stand when we want to walk and to walk when we want to run. 'Twas right what you said of the Fenians.

JACKSON What was that?

KATE They were misguided. They were trying to do too much. But they were good men, brave men, gallant men, and if they didn't make fools of themselves where would we be now?

[O'LEARY comes in.]

O'LEARY Where's Joan?

KATE Probably she's in her room. Don't disturb her.

O'LEARY Why not? She's after having some sort of fight with Coghlan.

---

60. *jigmareel* Figuratively, a wild goose chase. The word is made up of the names of two dances, the jig and the reel, so that "a jigmareel" is neither one thing nor the other.

KATE Ah, tell him have sense and have sense yourself. Can't you think what she'll have to face in the morning?

JACKSON Yes, Cady, leave the child alone. We don't know what goes on in the mind of a woman on an occasion like this.

O'LEARY Maybe you're right. That fellow Coghlan is very hard to get on with.

JACKSON You're lucky 'tis only a lover's tiff you have to trouble about, Cady. If you knew the temptation I went through tonight—

O'LEARY What temptation are you talking about, man?

JACKSON *[lightly, but with a sort of grim resolution]* When I came in here after being battered by those fellows. Do you know, Cady, if I was ten years younger, I'd have whipped her from under your eyes then if you were fifty times the man; ay, begod, I'd have captured her at the church door as they used to do in my grandfather's time, with fast horses and a brace of pistols.

O'LEARY *[delighted]* Well, well, well, that's a good one. That's a real good one! That's the best one yet! I can see you doing a lot of queer things, Corney, me ould flower, but if there's one thing I can't see you doing, 'tis making love to a woman. But, listen to me, listen here to me; to come back to serious things. Do you know what Jer Coghlan wants me to do?

JACKSON What, to double the dowry?

O'LEARY No, to stand.

JACKSON Stand as what?

O'LEARY As candidate of course.

JACKSON Anti-Parnellite?

O'LEARY Now, now, now, no ugly names. No ugly names! Mind you, if 'twas last month or last week even, I'd treat him with scorn, but now the Chief is gone—God rest his noble soul—we can leave bygones be bygones; and they want a real influential candidate to put up against that young whipper-snapper Hegarty. 'Twould be a great pleasure to myself to be able to do something for the country at last, and I know the English and their ways. They wouldn't fool me.

KATE Are you sure of that now?

O'LEARY Yerra, is it fool a butter-merchant? Sure, amn't I fooling them all my life? And another thing, 'twould be a great case for the band. They're eating their heads off for something to do.

JACKSON Well, do then, do. You won't do any harm.

O'LEARY Corney, you don't think they'd call me a turncoat? I couldn't bear anyone to call me a turncoat.

JACKSON Let them, man, let them. Don't they call me a Darwinist? Anyway, they're all turncoats now. They've forgotten long ago, all of them, what they were fighting about, and they're only fighting now because they like it.

O'LEARY Be the Lord above, Corney, that's a most remarkable statement. That's the best thing I heard said since the thing began. Listen, like a decent man, write it down for me and I'll fling it in their faces. They'll be so stupefied they won't be able to answer me. . . . Corney, *[with mounting fervour]* you're after taking a great load off my mind. What'll Hegarty say when he sees that? What can any of them say to it? Isn't it God's own Gospel truth that none of them had the sense to see? They're all turncoats, every man jack of them, and we may as well all turn our coats and be friends again. . . . I'll get rid of Jer Coghlan. I want to talk to you about me election address. Will you write it out for me, Corney, will you write it out for me?

JACKSON I will indeed—as a penance for my own foolishness.

O'LEARY I'll get rid of him, but I won't tell him that one. 'Twouldn't be in a Coghlan not to steal it. *[Exit.]*

KATE Did you mean that about Joan?

JACKSON I suppose you think I'm mad?

KATE Did you mean it, I said?

JACKSON I suppose it's part of the folly. St. Martin's Summer.[61] Ever since that night I've wanted her in a vague sort of way—in all the fights and speeches and demonstrations. And tonight when I came in and saw her, I felt that I was parting from life when I parted from her. I wanted her as I never wanted anything before. Forgive me, it's only an old man's fancy.

KATE You fool of hell, why didn't you tell me? Oh, what am I after doing?

---

61. *St. Martin's Summer.* Literally, Indian Summer, a warm period in the autumn. Figuratively, a return to the feelings of youth in middle age.

JACKSON   Why? You sound as though you were taking me seriously.

KATE   Man alive, you could have had her any time for the asking, and tonight—tonight, she'd have welcomed you like an angel of God.

JACKSON   Joan? Me? You're dreaming.

KATE   Ah, what dreaming? And now it's too late.

JACKSON   Too late? What do you mean too late? You're not in earnest.

[In the distance a door slams.]

KATE   Listen!

JACKSON   What?

KATE   Didn't you hear? Now?

JACKSON   I thought I heard a door closing.

KATE   You did.

JACKSON   But what—what does it mean?

KATE   It means Jer Coghlan's brats will never be able to call me a relation.

JACKSON   You mean Joan has hooked it?[62]

KATE   If she's the girl I think her, she's hooked it.

JACKSON   But how? Where?

KATE   Oh, she wouldn't be alone. Hurry! Hurry![63]

JACKSON   Do you mean she's gone off with that cub of a soldier?

KATE   Only you can stop her. She'll be heading for the station. For the love of God, Corney, go!

[JACKSON rushes out.]

KATE   *[hurrying to the window]* Mother of God, help him to bring her back!

[There is the noise of cheering in the distance. After a pause, O'LEARY comes in from the dining-room. He carries paper, pen and ink.]

O'LEARY   Where's Corney?

KATE   He's gone.

O'LEARY   Gone . . . Where's he gone? *[KATE doesn't reply.]* That's a fine thing to do to a man, and he after promising to help me write my election address. Did you hear them

---

62. *hooked it?* Run away.

63. The MS. ends here. The rest of the text has been reconstructed by Hugh Hunt for this edition.

cheering down the road? They'll be coming here in no time to bring me to the meeting, and Peter Hurley's after sending word he'll be bringing the band. What am I to do now? What in Heaven's name am I to do now? Wasn't I relying on Corney to give the start to my speech? *[He sits at the table with his papers.]* Oh Corney Jackson, Corney Jackson, you've let me down this time right enough.

KATE Corney's got more important things on his mind than your tomfoolery of a speech.

O'LEARY What d'ye mean, tomfoolery? Didn't Ned Coghlan say the Party's looking to me to be their candidate for the election?

KATE Is it to stand against Ned Hegarty and the Parnellites? God help you, man! You'll soon be forgetting which side you're fighting for.

O'LEARY Women! There's no woman born understands these things. Isn't Parnell dead, and the Fenians is finished? It's the duty of every man now to stand behind the clergy.

KATE If it's turncoats they want.

O'LEARY Turncoats! You'll use no such word in my house, or I'll turn you out in the street this night, if it's the last thing I do.

KATE I'll be going without your aid. Joan won't be needing me any more. It was for her sake, not yours, I came here.

O'LEARY It was a black and bitter day I took you under my roof.

[NELLIE comes in.]

NELLIE Father Henry's below with Mr. Coghlan, and there's a crowd outside to bring you to the meeting.

O'LEARY Tell them I'll be down in a minute. Tell them I'm after putting the last words to me grand speech on the future of Ireland.

NELLIE *[as she goes]* God help Ireland.

O'LEARY What's that she said? I'll stand no more of her impudence. God Almighty, is the two of you in league to thwart me? Out of this house she'll go at the end of the week, and not a penny more to her wages. Hasn't every thought gone out of me head with the two of yous? What was it Corney said? What the hell was it he said? . . . "They've forgotten what they were fighting about". . . . "They're only fighting

now because they like it." Oh, that's a good one! Wait now, till I put that down. . . . I wonder, though, would Father Henry like that? *[He scratches it out.]*
[From outside comes cries of "Speech!" "Cady O'Leary for Parliament!" Followed by cheers.]
D'ye hear that, woman? D'ye hear that? And you blethering about something more important. What's more important, can you tell me that?

KATE   Joan's gone.

O'LEARY   What's that you said?

KATE   Joan has left this house. She'll not be marrying Jer Coghlan or any of your gerrymandering politicians.[64]

O'LEARY   It's out of your mind, you are! Hasn't Father Henry persuaded the bishop himself to marry them tomorrow, and isn't the dowry all settled? Oh, they're a hard lot, the Coghlans, a mean, hard lot. But I bested them in the end.

KATE   I tell you Joan has gone. She's gone to find a life for herself; and, with God's help, she's gone with the right man.

O'LEARY   What man? . . . Gone where? Oh, I know well what you're after: it's to shame me in front of the Coghlans. But you'll not succeed, my lady! You'll not succeed! If Joan's reneged on me, I'll have the whole town searched from cellar to attic. She'll marry Jer Coghlan if I have to drag her to church on a hurdle.

[NELLIE comes in.]

NELLIE   What am I to do with that lot below? There's that Coghlan creature says he can't wait all night, and the old one is bothering the head off Father Henry, telling him the blight is at the potatoes, and Biddy Lally and Sorry Sullivan is in the kitchen drinking your whiskey.

O'LEARY   Is it to drive me out of my mind you want, the lot of you? Joan's gone, Corney's gone, my whiskey's gone, and now the mother's gone astray in her wits. . . . Here's my speech now, my lovely speech, without two sentences strung together. This is a fine way to treat a man has

---

64. *gerrymandering politicians.* Here, unscrupulous politicians. The word "gerrymander" derives from the name of Elbridge Gerry, a 19th-century Governor of Massachusetts who redrew electoral district boundaries to ensure his party's success, and thereby created an unlikely district which looked like a salamander on the map.

sacrificed his life to the cause of old Ireland. *[He gathers up his papers and goes.]*

NELLIE Dan Connors is back from the station, Miss. He said to tell you Miss Joan left town in the Dublin train.

KATE *[anxiously]* Did she say nothing to him, Nellie?

NELLIE She said to tell Miss Kate and Doctor Jackson she's gone to find her own happiness.

[It is growing dark in the room. The light from the torches outside flickers on the walls. KATE moves to the window.]

KATE *[to herself]* God grant she will! So, Corney, both of us failed her in the end.

NELLIE Did you say something, Miss?

KATE Ask Dan to come back in the morning to fetch away my trunk.

NELLIE Are you leaving us then?

KATE I am, Nellie. I'll be going back to the shop. Better I'd never left it.

NELLIE Would you take me with you, Miss?

KATE We'll see, Nellie, we'll see. This town is no place for the young. All that is young and beautiful is leaving Ireland now, like seagulls flying into the dark. It's a poor divided country we'll be from this night on.

[In the distance we hear the band approaching, playing "God Save Ireland".]

CURTAIN